The Sun Temple of Konark
A Chronicle in Stone

The Sun Temple of Konark
A Chronicle in Stone

Dr. Adyasha Das
Sareeta Pradhan
Dr. Anasuya Swain

BLACK EAGLE BOOKS
Dublin, USA | Bhubaneswar, India

 Black Eagle Books
USA address:
7464 Wisdom Lane
Dublin, OH 43016

India address:
E/312, Trident Galaxy, Kalinga Nagar,
Bhubaneswar-751003, Odisha, India

E-mail: info@blackeaglebooks.org
Website: www.blackeaglebooks.org

First International Edition Published by
Black Eagle Books, 2025

THE SUN TEMPLE OF KONARK: A CHRONICLE IN STONE
Dr. Adyasha Das
Sareeta Pradhan
Dr. Anasuya Swain

Copyright © **Dr. Adyasha Das | Sareeta Pradhan | Dr. Anasuya Swain**

All rights reserved. No part of this publication may be reproduced, stored in a retrieval system, or transmitted, in any form or by any means, electronic, mechanical, photocopying, recording or otherwise without the prior permission of the publisher.

Cover & Interior Design: Ezy's Publication

ISBN- 978-1-64560-771-7 (Paperback)

Printed in the United States of America

Dedication
For the chariot of the Sun, still moving,
still breathing, still teaching.

Contents

Foreword
  Konark Sun Temple: Art, Architecture
  and Living Heritage — 09

Chapter 1
  Introduction: The Sun Temple of Konark — 21

Chapter 2
  Historical Backdrop of Konark — 36

Chapter 3
  Architectural Features and Layout — 52

Chapter 4
  When the Stones Speak: Sculptural
  Treasures of Konark — 72

Chapter 5
  Conservation Strategies for the Sun Temple — 105

Chapter 6
  The Konark Dance Festival — 123

Chapter 7
  Circuits of Living Heritage — 153

  Bibliography — 180

Foreword

Konark Sun Temple: Art, Architecture, and Living Heritage

India's artistic and cultural heritage stands among the most profound legacies in the world, encompassing a confluence of spiritual symbolism, architectural excellence, and philosophical depth. Its influence extends far beyond geographical borders, earning global recognition through several UNESCO World Heritage Sites. One such marvel is the Konark Sun Temple, an architectural masterpiece that continues to mesmerize scholars, pilgrims, and travellers alike.

Situated on the eastern seaboard of India in Puri district, Odisha, about 65 kilometres from the state capital Bhubaneswar, the Konark Sun Temple stands as a monumental tribute to the Sun God, Surya. Despite the passage of centuries and the ravages of time, its artistic brilliance endures — a majestic reminder of Odisha's glorious past. Even in partial ruin, the temple's grandeur and sculptural finesse evoke awe and reverence. Commissioned by King Narasimhadeva I of the Eastern Ganga dynasty (1238–1264 CE), the temple was conceived not merely as a place of worship but as a symbol of royal might and divine authority. Historians continue to debate aspects of its chronology, purpose, and design, with interpretations ranging from political symbolism to astronomical and tantric significance.

European sailors, struck by its imposing dark stone silhouette against the sea, referred to it as the "Black Pagoda." Today, it remains one of the most visited and researched monuments in India — a testament to the creative genius of ancient Kalinga artisans.

A vast corpus of research has explored Konark from historical, archaeological, and artistic perspectives. Dr. Vikas Agrawal, in *The Konark Sun Temple*, presents a structural overview of the temple complex, decoding its architectural components and spatial organisation. Karuna Sagar Behera's 1995 work, *The Sun Temple of Konark: From Glory to its Fall*, offers an immersive narrative of the temple's creation, craftsmanship, and cultural essence, interwoven with rich visual documentation. Sanjay Baral, in *The Real History of Konark*, critically examines the temple's chronology, contesting the long-held belief that its construction belongs solely to the 13th century. He situates Konark within Odisha's sociopolitical and Buddhist milieu, enriching the historiographical discourse. The seminal work *New Light on the Sun Temple of Konarka* by Alice Boner and Sadasiva Rath Sarma introduces valuable translations of palm-leaf manuscripts, unearthing historical insights into the temple's rediscovery and partial restoration. The theory that the Sun Temple began as a Buddhist monument was proposed by Bishan Swarup in 1910. His claims were based on the temple's potential connection to a mythical "Maitreya Vana" and a few symbols he interpreted as Buddhist. However, these claims have been strongly refuted by historians and archaeologists.

Inter-alia, these studies illuminate Konark's multidimensional significance — as an artistic phenomenon, a site of worship, and a subject of mythic imagination.

Konark's genesis is steeped in legend and devotion. As per traditional accounts, the temple was constructed under the royal directive of Narasimhadeva I, mobilising over a thousand artisans over twelve years. The poignant tale of Dharmapada, the young son of chief architect Bisu Maharana, who solved an architectural impasse but sacrificed himself to preserve the sanctity of the shrine, forms an inseparable part of the temple's lore. This legend symbolises the eternal human yearning for perfection and the divine. Karuna Sagar Behera observes that a tale resembling the Dharmapada legend is also connected with the Varaha Narasingha Temple at Simanchalam, though the central figure bears a different name. He mentions that the name Dharmapada itself was later introduced by Pandit Gopabandhu. Historical accounts indicate that the artisans faced tremendous pressure when the king advanced the consecration date to coincide with a Chandrabhaga Snana Yatra. The challenge of raising and placing the colossal Amalaka Shila and Kalasha atop the temple may have inspired this dramatic legend, though it lacks historical authenticity. Still, the narrative reflects that around 1,200 craftsmen laboured for twelve years near a water body, remaining away from their homes to bring the temple to completion. Scholars such as James Harle have reconstructed the original plan — consisting of two main components, the Rekha Deul (sanctum tower) and the Jagamohana (assembly hall). The towering sanctum, once rising to nearly 70 metres, collapsed around the 16th century, leaving the Jagamohana and Nata Mandapa as its principal surviving structures.

Konark epitomises the zenith of Kalinga architecture, a refined expression of the Nagara style. Rooted in the northern Indian Nagara tradition, the temple features the characteristic deul (sanctum tower) and jagamohana (assembly hall), both richly adorned with intricate carvings of deities, celestial beings, and scenes from daily life. Conceived as the colossal chariot of Surya, the temple is drawn by seven galloping horses and mounted on twenty-four intricately carved wheels, each representing the solar cycle — twelve months, eight prahars (divisions of the day), and the ceaseless motion of time. Every element in the temple's design communicates a symbolic vocabulary — lions trampling elephants to depict the conquest of power and wealth, erotic figures illustrating the fullness of life, and celestial deities embodying cosmic order. The play of sunlight across the sanctum throughout the day mirrors the Sun's journey across the heavens, reaffirming the temple's profound astronomical alignment.

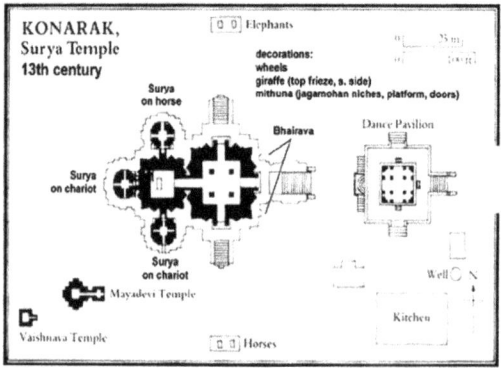

Plan of Konark Sun Temple by Percy Brown (Photo courtesy Swathi Gopalakrishnan)

Constructed primarily with khondalite, laterite, and chlorite, the monument reflects an extraordinary technical achievement for its time. Ancient texts and oral traditions suggest the use of magnetic and metallurgical principles in the temple's structure, possibly creating electromagnetic effects that inspired later myths about the "floating idol of Surya". Surrounding the main shrine are auxiliary monuments — the Chhayadevi Temple, Vaishnava Temple, community kitchen, and wells — each revealing the pluralistic spirit of Konark. These smaller shrines demonstrate the complex integrated multiple Hindu traditions, transcending sectarian boundaries. The Chhayadevi Temple, likely predating the main sanctum, is an exquisite repository of iconography, while the Vaishnava Temple signifies the temple's inclusivity, acknowledging the Vaishnavite and Saura faiths alike.

Chhaya Devi Temple Wall

Behind the grand Konark Sun Temple stands the Chhaya Devi or Maya Devi Temple, which scholars identify as the site of the earlier Sun shrine, later expanded into the monumental structure we see today. This older temple, smaller in scale yet rich in artistry, once housed three

Parswadevata sculptures on its sides. The surviving southern image, though severely damaged by invaders, still reveals traces of its original magnificence, albeit simpler than those of the later temple. The temple walls display finely carved figures of women, elephants, horses, and deities such as Surya, Vayu, Agni, and Vishnu, attesting to the artistic excellence of the period. Its unique waterspouts, shaped like crocodiles and yali (mythical beasts) and sculpted from chlorite stone, further enhance its architectural charm. The porch interiors too are adorned with delicate and detailed carvings, preserving the memory of a glorious artistic legacy that predated the celebrated Sun Temple.

Chhaya Devi Temple

By the 17th century, the once-majestic structure had succumbed to natural decay and human neglect. Theories about its collapse range from seismic disturbances and magnetic destabilisation to invasions and stone pilferage. In the early 20th century, under the direction of the Archaeological Survey of India, major conservation efforts began. In 1903, the Jagamohana was filled with sand to prevent further collapse, and surrounding structures were stabilised. Since then, the ASI has continued systematic restoration and preservation work. In 2022, the ASI initiated a historic project to carefully remove the sand from the Jagamohana, introducing stainless-steel support systems for long-term stability — a landmark step in the temple's modern conservation history.

Konark in the Modern Context: Tourism, Heritage, and Sustainability

Today, the Konark Sun Temple stands not only as a vestige of medieval Odisha's architectural prowess but also as a vibrant node in India's cultural tourism network. Featured prominently in the Odisha Heritage Circuit, Golden Triangle (Bhubaneswar–Puri–Konark), and Eco-Spiritual Tourism Circuits, Konark bridges history, mythology, and community identity.

The Konark Dance Festival and International Sand Art Festival, held annually near the temple, have revitalised the site's cultural resonance, drawing global audiences and promoting traditional Odishan arts. The monument also plays a key role in community-based tourism initiatives, supporting local artisans, guides, and craftspersons.

Future-focused heritage management plans advocate

for sustainable tourism models — emphasising controlled visitor flow, digital interpretation, heritage trails linking Raghurajpur (craft village) and Chilika Lake, and climate-resilient conservation measures. Such integrated planning ensures that Konark continues to inspire, educate, and economically empower future generations.

Konark is more than stone and sculpture — it is an architectural hymn to the cosmic order, translating metaphysical thought into material splendour. Its sundial precision, geometric balance, and sculptural language embody a synthesis of art, science, and spirituality. The temple's inclusion on India's currency note and its poetic celebration by Rabindranath Tagore — *"Here the language of stone surpasses the language of man"* — affirm its immortal stature in India's civilizational narrative.

The Konark Sun Temple remains a timeless dialogue between light and stone, divinity and human creativity. From its medieval inception to its modern conservation, Konark mirrors the resilience of Indian heritage itself — ever luminous, ever alive. As India crafts its new tourism circuits under evolving heritage policies, Konark emerges as a keystone of cultural continuity, embodying the essence of responsible tourism, community engagement, and sustainable preservation. Its story — from construction to rediscovery — is not merely history, but a living lesson in how civilizations honour their past while envisioning a conscious, inclusive, and radiant future.

This book offers a nuanced and interdisciplinary study of the Konark Sun Temple, blending historical inquiry with a forward-looking perspective on its evolving significance within contemporary cultural and tourism frameworks.

While firmly grounded in the architectural, iconographic, and spiritual dimensions of this UNESCO World Heritage Site, the volume extends its focus to the emerging paradigms of heritage management, cultural sustainability, and experiential tourism that are reshaping the way such monuments are perceived and engaged within the modern era.

A distinctive contribution of this work lies in its emphasis on tourism potential and circuit development as instruments of both preservation and progress. The study positions Konark not as an isolated architectural marvel, but as an integral node within Odisha's Golden Triangle—Bhubaneswar, Puri, and Konark,each site reflecting a continuum of religious, artistic, and socio-cultural evolution. In addition, it highlights the scope of integrating lesser-known heritage sites such as Chaurasi, Kuruma, Beleswar, and Balighai into extended heritage circuits, thereby fostering regional connectivity and diversified visitor experiences.

Drawing upon comparative examples from Indian and Southeast Asian heritage circuits, the book argues for the adoption of sustainable and community-based tourism models that align conservation with livelihood generation. It underscores the potential of interpretive heritage trails, digital documentation, craft-based tourism, and eco-cultural initiatives near Chandrabhaga and the marine-drive-corridor, situating Konark within broader discourses on environmental stewardship and responsible tourism.

By combining archaeological depth with applied foresight, this work contributes meaningfully to scholarship on heritage tourism and cultural policy. It will serve as a valuable resource for academics, heritage professionals, tourism planners, policymakers, and students seeking to understand how ancient monuments like Konark can evolve into dynamic centres of cultural learning and sustainable tourism in the twenty-first century.

Before embarking on my own writing on the Konark Sun Temple, I immersed myself in an extensive body of literature by celebrated historians, art critics, archaeologists, and writers who have explored India's architectural and cultural legacy from multiple perspectives. These readings enriched my understanding of sacred architecture, temple symbolism, and the evolution of religious aesthetics across centuries. Yet, among all the works I encountered, none influenced me as profoundly as Shilapadma, the Odia novel by my mother, Jnanpith awardee Dr. Pratibha Ray, and its English translation, Citadel of Love. Set against the backdrop of the construction of the Konark Sun Temple, the novel masterfully intertwines historical imagination with spiritual introspection, portraying the human emotions, creative zeal, and divine aspiration that shaped this monumental creation. Through its vivid portrayal of characters, the narrative transcends time, offering a deeply human understanding of devotion, art, and sacrifice. Reading Shilapadma not only illuminated for me the philosophical and emotional dimensions of Konark but also inspired me to explore the site beyond its stones and sculptures—to see it as a living symbol of artistic transcendence and human endeavour.

I extend my sincere gratitude to Satya Pattanaik, Director, *Black Eagle Books*, USA, for his continued faith in my work and for supporting the publication of this book. His unwavering encouragement and commitment to promoting my writings have been invaluable. I feel deeply honoured

that six of my books published by *Black Eagle Books* have featured on the Amazon Bestseller list. My heartfelt thanks also go to Ashok Parida of *BEB* for his aesthetic sense and artistic brilliance in designing the book's cover and layout.

I owe special gratitude to Sankar Narayan Mallik, whose meticulous reading of the manuscript and insightful editorial guidance greatly enriched the final work. His expertise and cooperation in my literary pursuits have been a constant source of strength and inspiration.

My deepest appreciation also goes to my co-authors — **Mrs. S. Pradhan**, Assistant Professor, IITTM Bhubaneswar, and **Ms. Anasuya Swain**, Research Scholar and Visiting Faculty, IITTM Bhubaneswar — for their sincerity, diligence, and collaborative spirit. Working alongside them, sharing ideas, and engaging in field visits made this project a truly enriching experience. Grateful thanks to Ashutosh Baral and Priyabarat Shial for their invaluable support and assistance during our field visits and photo shoots.

To my cherished readers, I express my heartfelt thanks for your steadfast support, affection, and enthusiasm. Your loyal readership has not only brought my books to the bestseller charts but also made every word I write feel worthwhile. Your thoughtful reviews, reflections, and discussions continue to inspire and motivate me to explore new creative horizons and strive for excellence in every endeavour.

"A tribute to the unknown architects, masons, and sculptors of Konark—creators of a unparallelled testament in stone."

Dr. Adyasha Das

Introduction: The Sun Temple of Konark

Indian art and culture are among the richest and most diverse cultural expressions in the world. The timeless appeal of India's spiritual heritage, architectural magnificence, and sculptural finesse has captivated the global imagination. Many of India's historic sites have been recognized by UNESCO as World Heritage Sites, owing to their universal value, cultural richness, and historical significance. Among them stands the Konark Sun Temple—a resplendent gem of Odishan architecture that epitomizes the apex of medieval Indian temple design and devotion.

A Monument Beyond Time

Situated on the eastern coast of India in the Puri district of Odisha, about 65 kilometres from Bhubaneswar and 35 kilometres northeast of Puri town, the Sun Temple of Konark rises in grandeur and symbolism. Erected in the 13th century CE, this majestic temple is dedicated to Surya, the Hindu sun god, and is renowned for its architectural brilliance and intricate stone carvings. Even in its ruined state, the temple's magnificence is awe-inspiring and continues to draw scholars, pilgrims, and tourists alike. Known as the "Black Pagoda" by European sailors due to its dark hue and navigational prominence, Konark was once an important trading port. It is believed to be situated on an ancient site of sun worship, referred to in Indian texts as Arka-Kshetra and Kainapara. This religious association, coupled with its coastal prominence, made Konark a fitting place for building a grand temple to the solar deity.

The Konark Sun Temple is widely considered the pinnacle of Kalinga architecture, a distinctive style that evolved in ancient Odisha. Conceived as a colossal chariot of the Sun god, the temple is a marvel of creative imagination and engineering. The complex consists of the Deula (sanctum), the Jagamohana (assembly hall), and the Natamandira (dancing hall), all aligned on an east-west axis to catch the first rays of the rising sun.

The temple is built in the form of a 24-wheeled chariot, drawn by seven horses, symbolizing the days of the week and hours of the day. Each wheel is a masterpiece of stone sculpture, intricately carved with motifs of daily life, celestial beings, animals, and erotic scenes. The erotic sculptures, comparable to those at Khajuraho, speak of a philosophical worldview that embraced sensuality as a divine expression of life and cosmic energy. As observed by Percy Brown, the Konark temple is the "grandest achievement of the eastern school of architecture," and represents the culmination of temple-building activities in medieval Odisha.

The temple was built by King Narasimhadeva I of the Eastern Ganga Dynasty in the mid-13th century, most likely following his military victory over Tughral Tughan Khan, the Governor of Bengal under the Delhi Sultanate. Multiple historical and textual sources including the Madala Panji, Katakarajavamsavali, and Ganga Vamsanucharita affirm his role in commissioning this monumental structure as an offering to Surya. The copper plate charter of 1295 CE (Saka year 1217) describes the temple as a divine abode where the Sun god resides with other deities.

Both academic and popular writings discuss the enduring legend of a floating Surya idol at Konark, believed to have been suspended by a massive lodestone magnet. According to popular belief, the magnet's force disrupted ships' compasses, prompting its removal and causing the idol to fall or be lost to the sea. However, scholars find no historical evidence supporting this tale, viewing it instead as a later myth possibly inspired by the temple's coastal location and magnetic properties. Academic studies focus on the temple's architecture, iconography, engineering, and historical context, often clarifying misconceptions and emphasizing that the so-called magnetic levitation of the idol remains unsubstantiated.

Legend has it that 1,200 masons laboured for twelve years, using twelve years' worth of the kingdom's revenue to complete the temple—a testament to the immense resources and devotion poured into its making. Folk tales embellish the story with the poignant legend of Dharmapada, a prodigious young boy who sacrificed his life for the completion of the temple's crown stone, a story that adds a layer of spiritual martyrdom to the monument. Konark has always been more than just an architectural marvel. It is part of the sacred Golden Triangle of Odisha, along with Puri (home to the Jagannath Temple) and Bhubaneswar (the Temple City), forming a triad of spiritual energy and sacred geography. Each year, thousands gather for the Chandrabhaga Mela, a religious festival celebrating the Sun god, held near the now-vanished Chandrabhaga River. The site continues to be a pilgrimage destination, where the ruins themselves exude sanctity.

Despite its grandeur, much of the temple lies in ruins today, and the reasons for its collapse remain a matter of speculation. Scholars such as Donaldson and Panigrahi debate whether natural calamities, iconoclasm, or structural failure contributed to its destruction. Restoration and preservation efforts have been underway since the colonial period, and the Archaeological Survey of India (ASI) continues to maintain the site. Yet, even in its ruin, Konark transcends time. As art historian Ananda Coomaraswamy once said, the temple remains "one of the noblest monuments of Indian medieval art."

The Konark Sun Temple is a UNESCO World Heritage Site since 1984, recognized for its "outstanding universal value" as a masterwork of human creative genius. The iconography, structural innovation, and cultural symbolism embedded in its stones reflect not only a regional artistic zenith but also a universal human aspiration—to capture the divine in form and function. The Konark Sun Temple, one of the grandest architectural marvels of medieval India, has captivated historians, archaeologists, and scholars for centuries. Over the years, multiple scholars have examined the temple's architectural grandeur, socio-political context, and enigmatic fall, contributing significantly to our understanding of this UNESCO World Heritage Site.

Dr. Vikas Agrawal, in his book The Konark Sun Temple, presents a structured and systematic account of the various components of the temple complex. His study highlights the layout, iconographic significance, and symbolic resonance of the structures within the temple precincts. Agrawal meticulously details the orientation of the temple, its alignment with solar movement, and the metaphysical symbolism embedded in the sculptural narratives.

Karuna Sagar Behera, in his authoritative work The Sun Temple of Konark: From Glory to Its Fall (1995), offers a comprehensive chronicle of the temple's architectural splendour and historical trajectory. Behera delves into both the religious and cultural symbolism of the temple, analyzing the sculptural sophistication, tantric motifs, and exquisite stonework that define its uniqueness. His book also includes illustrations that vividly recreate the original magnificence of the now-ruined structure. Behera's work draws attention to the interplay of mythology and history, as well as the engineering marvels employed during its construction.

Sanjay Baral, in The Real History of Konark, ventures into unresolved debates surrounding the temple's dating and origin. While the mainstream view attributes the temple to the 13th century under Narasimhadeva I, Baral questions whether its foundation may have been laid earlier. His research situates the construction within the socio-political and religious context of Odisha in the 13th century. Interestingly, he explores the Buddhist influences in the region, raising questions about possible syncretic elements in the temple's iconography and design.

New Light on the Sun Temple of Konarka by Alice Boner and Sadasiva Rath Sarma is a pathbreaking contribution that illuminates the process of restoration and rediscovery. The book reveals how the temple, buried for nearly 300 years under dense jungle, re-emerged to the world, posing immense challenges to scholars and conservationists. Their work includes English translations of rare palm-leaf manuscripts, offering insights into rituals, measurements, and legends that surround the temple. Boner, known for her mathematical analysis of temple architecture, also interprets sacred geometry and canonical proportions used in Konark's design.

A tinted lithograph of a image of the Surya Temple at Konarak, Orissa. Drawn by James Fergusson and lithoed by T C Dibdin. © The Trustees of the British Museum

Historical Context and the Legend of Dharmapada

Historical evidence suggests that the construction of Konark was initiated by King Narasimhadeva I as an assertion of dynastic authority. According to New World Encyclopedia, the project engaged a workforce of over 1,200 artisans and architects, and the king is believed to have spent the equivalent of twelve years of state revenue to see the project to completion. The famed legend of Dharmapada, the young son of the chief architect Bisu Maharana, adds a layer of poignant mysticism to the story. As the construction neared its deadline, the architects faced a critical engineering impasse—the placement of the final capping stone. Dharmapada, merely 12 years old yet deeply learned in temple architecture, solved the problem and placed the stone, thus securing the structure. However, fearing that his success would bring dishonor to the senior architects and violate royal protocol, he leapt to his death from the temple's top. This self-sacrifice, as the legend goes, rendered the temple ritually unfit for consecration, and Surya was never formally worshipped there.

Architectural Decline and Collapse

The Konark Sun Temple once stood as a towering symbol of Odisha's architectural glory. Modelled as a colossal chariot of the Sun God Surya, it was renowned for its intricate carvings, astronomical alignments, and grand scale. However, despite its robust foundations and ingenious design, the temple's architectural integrity began to deteriorate by the late medieval period. According to James Harle, a leading art historian, the original temple complex consisted of two principal structures: the main sanctum (deul) and the dancing hall (natya mandapa). While the mandapa still stands, the towering deul collapsed—likely in the late 16th century or thereafter. Though some early historians speculated that the temple remained incomplete due to the premature death of the king, this theory lacks substantial archaeological backing. Natural decay, salt-laden

winds from the Bay of Bengal, and long periods of neglect contributed to the ruin of this once-magnificent solar shrine.
- Collapse of the Deul (Main Sanctum)
  The original temple complex comprised three primary structures:
- The main sanctum (deul) — over 60 meters high.
- The jagamohana (assembly hall) — which still stands.
- The natya mandapa (dance hall) — now in ruins.

The deul collapsed sometime between the 16th and 17th centuries. Although theories vary, the exact cause remains elusive. Early colonial accounts mention a ruined structure already buried under sand and vegetation, suggesting that the collapse was not sudden but the result of gradual degradation.

Factors Contributing to Architectural Decline

Environmental Exposure: The temple's coastal location exposed it to strong saline winds from the Bay of Bengal, which slowly corroded the chlorite and laterite stones. The absence of maintenance during periods of political instability hastened its decay.

Seismic Activity and Structural Imbalance: Though there is no direct record of a major earthquake, scholars like James Harle have suggested that minor seismic activity or foundational imbalance might have contributed to the collapse of the towering deul.

Incompletion Theories: Some early theories proposed that the temple was never completed due to the untimely death of King Narasimhadeva I. However, this remains speculative and unsupported by strong archaeological evidence.

Human Intervention: Historical evidence suggests that iron clamps and dowels used to bind the massive stone blocks were removed by British colonists and local looters, which may have weakened the structural integrity.

Neglect and Sand Encroachment: Over time, the temple was abandoned and buried under layers of sand and dense forest cover. The lack of continuous ritual worship and state patronage led to centuries of neglect.

Contemporary Challenges and Preservation Issues

Despite its UNESCO World Heritage status, the Konark Sun Temple continues to face multiple conservation challenges in the modern era:

- Erosion and Weathering

The surviving stone surfaces are highly vulnerable to weathering.

Moisture and salt-laden air continue to erode delicate carvings.

Biological growth (like moss and lichen) damages the stonework.

- Water Seepage and Foundation Instability

Water accumulation around the foundation has raised concerns about the stability of the Jagamohana, which was filled with sand by the British in the early 20th century to prevent collapse. There is ongoing debate about whether the sand inside the Jagamohana should be removed or retained.

- Tourism Pressure

With over hundreds of thousands of visitors annually, footfall stress, vibrations, and pollution are constant threats. Lack of regulated crowd control sometimes leads to damage to carvings and heritage structures.

- **Lack of Advanced Conservation Techniques**

The use of traditional vs. modern conservation methods is a point of contention. There is a shortage of trained conservation artisans capable of working on such intricate heritage structures.

Insufficient Documentation and Digital Archiving: Though some digital models and 3D scanning have been initiated, systematic documentation of every stone and sculpture is still incomplete.

Encroachments and Commercialization: The area surrounding the temple faces encroachment from vendors and unregulated commercial activities, which disrupts the sanctity and aesthetics of the site.

Sun Temples in Other Civilizations - Comparison with the Konark Sun Temple

Worship of the Sun as a life-giving and celestial force has been a common religious and cultural motif across ancient civilizations. From the Americas to Mesopotamia, and from Egypt to East Asia, solar deities were often placed at the apex of pantheons, symbolizing kingship, power, regeneration, and cosmic order. Temples dedicated to the Sun thus became focal points of spiritual and political life.

Ancient Egypt – The Sun Temples of Heliopolis: In ancient Egypt, the Sun god Ra (or Re) occupied a central position in the religious worldview. The Sun temples at Heliopolis, particularly under the Old Kingdom Pharaohs such as Userkaf and Niuserre, were monumental complexes built not with traditional enclosed sanctuaries but open-air altars to allow direct exposure to sunlight. These temples featured obelisks, solar altars, and sun boats—

symbolizing the solar journey through the sky and the underworld. While few structures survive, inscriptions and archaeological remnants underscore their ritual significance and cosmological function.

Inca Civilization – The Coricancha (Qorikancha) Temple, Peru: In the capital city of Cusco, the Coricancha temple was the most sacred site in the Inca Empire, dedicated to Inti, the Sun god. The temple was richly adorned with gold, symbolizing the solar radiance, and served as a ceremonial centre for solstices and agricultural festivals. Its architectural alignment ensured the penetration of sunlight into its inner sanctum during key astronomical events. The Spaniards later built the Church of Santo Domingo over its ruins, but remnants of its precision stone masonry and sacred layout endure.

Mesopotamia – Solar Worship in Sippar: In ancient Mesopotamia, particularly in the city of Sippar, the Sun god Shamash was venerated in grand ziggurats and temples. Though not entirely open to the sky like Egyptian examples, these temples often featured high terraces to facilitate interaction with the divine light. Shamash was considered the deity of justice and divine order, and his temple rituals emphasized moral and legal oversight.

Japan – The Ise Grand Shrine: Although not a temple in the classical architectural sense, the Ise Grand Shrine in Japan is dedicated to Amaterasu, the Sun goddess and mythological progenitor of the Japanese imperial family. Rebuilt every 20 years in keeping with Shinto principles of ritual renewal, the shrine's design evokes natural harmony and solar veneration, though lacking the monumental scale of stone temples found elsewhere.

Comparison with the Konark Sun Temple

The Konark Sun Temple, constructed in the 13th century CE by King Narasimhadeva I of the Eastern Ganga dynasty, stands as a unique synthesis of monumental architecture, iconography, astronomical alignment, and solar symbolism in India.Unlike the open-air solar temples of Egypt or the stepped platforms of Sippar, Konark is conceived as a colossal stone chariot of Surya, drawn by seven horses on twelve intricately carved wheels. This metaphorical representation is unmatched in global sun-temple architecture, highlighting an integration of myth, function, and geometry.

Like the Inca Coricancha, Konark is also aligned to solar movements. The main sanctum (now in ruins) was oriented so that the first rays of the rising sun would illuminate the presiding deity. This solar alignment, paired with the temple's intricate sculptural program, positions it as both a cosmic observatory and a devotional site.

Ritual Function and Aesthetic Embellishment:
While temples such as Heliopolis and Coricancha were primarily ritualistic centres with relatively simple structures, Konark combines religious function with elaborate visual narrative. The sculptures on its walls depict divine beings, dancers, animals, and erotic couples, reflecting the Tantric integration of sacred and sensual, body and cosmos—something less pronounced in other traditions.

Material and Durability:
Konark, built of chlorite, laterite, and khondalite stone, has endured as a physical monument despite partial

collapse, unlike the mostly vanished Egyptian Sun temples. The artistic finesse of its carvings also differentiates it from the plainer construction of other sun temples.

While solar worship is a universal phenomenon, the Konark Sun Temple represents a particularly sophisticated and symbolic expression of solar devotion. In terms of artistic grandeur, architectural imagination, and astronomical precision, it surpasses many of its global counterparts. Konark is not only a place of worship but a cosmogram carved in stone—where the journey of the sun across the sky is translated into a dynamic spiritual and artistic experience

The Aim of This Book

This book presents a critical and in-depth study of the Konark Sun Temple, with a focus on its aesthetic, architectural, and symbolic dimensions. Engaging with a range of disciplinary perspectives, the work synthesizes insights from classical Sanskrit and Odia texts, contemporary scholarship, vernacular folklore, and ethnographic fieldwork to construct a holistic understanding of the site's historical and cultural significance.

Konark is examined not merely as a monumental relic of the thirteenth century, but as a dynamic site of meaning-making—where cosmological principles, ritual practices, and artistic expression intersect. The temple's architectural schema and sculptural programme are analysed in relation to broader Indic traditions of temple-building, solar worship, and tantric cosmology, situating Konark within the continuum of sacred architecture in South Asia.

In addition to its religious and artistic import, the book addresses Konark's designation as a UNESCO World

Heritage Site and interrogates its role in the contemporary cultural economy. It examines patterns of heritage tourism and emerging tourist typologies, including experiential, cultural, and responsible tourism. Emphasis is placed on the temple's contribution to sustainable livelihoods, local entrepreneurship, and community-based conservation initiatives. By contextualizing Konark within current debates on heritage management, cultural sustainability, and tourism policy, this study seeks to bridge the gap between academic inquiry and applied heritage discourse. Ultimately, the work positions the Konark Sun Temple as not only a masterpiece of medieval Indian architecture, but also as an enduring symbol of cultural resilience and socio-economic potential in the twenty-first century.

The book unfolds the multifaceted story of the Konark Sun Temple through a sequence of interconnected chapters that explore its history, architecture, art, and living heritage. The opening chapter introduces the grandeur and significance of the Sun Temple, setting the tone for a deeper understanding of its cultural and spiritual essence. The following chapter traces the ancient history of Konark, situating the temple within its historical, dynastic, and mythological contexts. The architectural and sculptural chapters examine the temple's unique design, engineering mastery, and the magnificent carvings that make it a marvel of creativity. A dedicated chapter on conservation discusses the challenges and strategies involved in preserving this UNESCO World Heritage Site. The narrative then moves to the vibrant present with a chapter on the Konark Dance Festival, a celebration that revives the temple's artistic legacy. The final chapter, Circuits of Living Heritage, expands the perspective beyond the monument, highlighting Konark's connection to surrounding heritage sites and its evolving role in cultural tourism. Together, these chapters offer a comprehensive exploration of Konark — as both a masterpiece of the past and a living symbol of India's enduring artistic spirit.

References
- Behera, K.S. (1993). *Konark: The Heritage City*. Bhubaneswar.
- Behera, K.S. (2005). *Art and Architecture of Konark*. New Delhi.
- Brown, Percy (1965). *Indian Architecture (Buddhist and Hindu Period)*. Bombay: D.B. Taraporevala Sons.
- Coomaraswamy, Ananda K. (1911). "Mediaeval Sinhalese Art". London.
- Davidson, Linda Kay and Gitlitz, David M. (2002). *Pilgrimage: From the Ganges to Graceland*. Santa Barbara.
- Donaldson, T. E. (1985, 1986, 2005). *Hindu Temple Art of Orissa*, Vols. I & II. Leiden.
- Helaine, Silverman (2008). *Intangible Heritage Embodied*. Springer.
- Mitra, Debala (1998). *Konark*. Archaeological Survey of India.
- Mohapatra, R.P. (1982, 1989). *Archaeology in Odisha*. Bhubaneswar.
- Panigrahi, K.C. (1957). *History of Orissa*. Cuttack.
- Pradhan, R. (2012). *Temple Legends of Odisha*. Bhubaneswar.
- Richard Carnac Temple, ed. (1911). *The Legends of the Punjab*. London.
- Stirling, Andrew (1825). *Account of Orissa*. Calcutta.
- *Journal of the Asiatic Society of Bengal* (JASB), 1896.
- ShodhKosh: Journal of Visual and Performing Arts.

Historical Backdrop of Konark

To understand Konark is to journey through the layered sands of time—where myth blends with history, and dynasties rise and fall, leaving behind fragments of stone, scripture, and legend. Long before the Sun Temple emerged as a beacon of architectural brilliance, this region had already witnessed centuries of political shifts, religious evolution, maritime enterprise, and cultural confluence.

This chapter traces the ancient roots of Konark through the lens of successive dynasties that shaped the region's identity—from the early rulers of Kalinga to the Mahameghavahanas, Sailodbhavas, Bhauma-Karas, Somavamsis, and ultimately, the Eastern Gangas. It explores how this coastal expanse, once known as Mitravana and Uddiyanaka, evolved into a sacred and strategic space, deeply entwined with Sun worship, Buddhist philosophy, maritime trade, and temple patronage.

Far from being an isolated monument, the Sun Temple of Konark is the culmination of a long civilizational process. The historical narrative that follows provides the foundational context for understanding how the soil of Konark was fertilized with myth, power, faith, and artistic aspiration—long before its stones were set in place. History is the chronological record of human existence and its events. A smoothly functioning society requires a framework for understanding past events and guiding present actions. Antiquities, literature, inscriptions, coins—these sources of history serve as guiding lights for intellectuals, society, and reformers. By interpreting these sources, we gain insights into the past, information for the present, and measures for future development.

Konark, a historic town in the Indian state of Odisha, is best known for the magnificent Sun Temple, an architectural marvel that reflects the rich cultural and artistic heritage of ancient India. The origins of Konark trace back to the early medieval period, with significant historical and mythological associations. The town derives its name from the Sanskrit words *Kona* (corner) and *Arka* (Sun), indicating its connection to sun worship. Konark has been associated with Hindu mythology, particularly with the worship of Surya, the Sun God. According to ancient texts and local legends, the Sun Temple was originally conceived by Lord Krishna's son, Samba. It is believed that Samba was afflicted with leprosy due to a curse from his father. Seeking redemption, he performed rigorous penance for twelve years near the banks of the Chandrabhaga River, where he ultimately built the first Sun Temple after being cured by Surya.

Konark continues to be a major pilgrimage centre, attracting devotees and historians alike. The annual Konark Dance Festival, held in the backdrop of the temple ruins, celebrates the region's artistic traditions, keeping its legacy alive. Konark, renowned today for its magnificent Sun Temple, has a history that extends far beyond the medieval period. Various sources, including archaeological excavations, ancient literature, numismatic evidence, inscriptions, and historical monuments, provide insight into Konark's antiquity. These sources indicate that Konark was an important religious and cultural hub long before the construction of the Sun Temple in the 13th century A.D.

Archaeological discoveries at Manikapatna, an ancient port near Konark, suggest that the region was inhabited as early as the 2nd century B.C. Excavations have revealed Neolithic pottery fragments and Celts, pointing to early human settlements. These findings indicate that Konark had cultural and trade links with other civilizations, possibly engaging in maritime trade with Southeast Asia.

In the 7th century A.D., the Chinese traveller I-tsing mentioned Konark in his travel accounts, highlighting its significance as a centre of learning and spirituality. By the 9th and 10th centuries, Buddhism flourished in the region, as evidenced by the Buddhist monastery at Kuruma, located just 8 km from Konark. This site contains remnants of Buddhist stupas and images of Lord Buddha in the Bhumisparsha Mudra, signifying its importance as a pilgrimage centre during the period.

Ancient literary texts also provide references to *Konark's* prominence. The *Brahmanda Purana*, one of the major *Puranas*, mentions the worship of the Sun God in this region. Similarly, *Buddhist Jataka tales* narrate stories of Sun worship, indicating the region's religious traditions even before the rise of the Eastern Ganga dynasty. The *Madalapanji, the* chronicle of the *Jagannath* Temple in Puri, and the *Samba Purana*, dedicated to the worship of Surya (the Sun God), reinforce the belief that *Konark* had been a sacred site for centuries.

Konark as a Centre for Sun Worship

Long before the construction of the famous Sun Temple by King Narasimhadeva I in the 13th century, Konark was already a major centre for Sun worship. The reverence for the Sun God, known as Surya Narayana, has deep roots in India's religious traditions, particularly in the coastal regions of Odisha. The Puranas and ancient inscriptions describe the existence of smaller shrines dedicated to Surya in and around Konark, suggesting that the grand temple built later was a culmination of an already established tradition.

According to the Samba Purana, Samba, the son of Lord Krishna, is believed to have established a Sun temple at Mitravana—widely identified with present-day Konark. This ancient text narrates his story and underscores Konark's enduring sanctity as a revered centre of Sun worship. Additionally, historical texts suggest that Konark was an important maritime and trade hub in ancient times. Its location near the Bay of Bengal made it a crucial point for coastal trade with Southeast Asia. Many historians believe that sailors and merchants paid homage to the Sun God at Konark before embarking on their sea voyages.

Rise of the Eastern Gangas and the 13th-Century Transformation

The historical significance of Konark reached its peak under the Eastern Ganga dynasty (11th–15th centuries A.D.), particularly during the reign of King Narasimhadeva I (1238–1264 A.D.). His grand vision to construct an architectural masterpiece dedicated to the Sun God resulted in the Konark Sun Temple, a marvel of engineering and artistry. This temple, designed in the shape of a colossal chariot with 24 intricately carved wheels, symbolized the cosmic journey of the Sun God.

The construction of the Sun Temple not only reinforced Konark's status as a religious centre but also marked the culmination of its centuries-old tradition of Sun worship. The temple served as a spiritual and cultural beacon, attracting pilgrims, scholars, and artisans from far and wide.

The region's prominence in religious and cultural activities likely contributed to its selection as the site for the Sun Temple Konark which remains a symbol of Odisha's artistic excellence and spiritual legacy. The site was declared a UNESCO World Heritage Site in 1984, recognizing its cultural and historical significance. Today, the Sun Temple stands as a testament to ancient India's architectural prowess and devotion to Surya.

Kalinga was ruled by the Sailodbhava dynasty by 6th and 7th century, as evidenced by copper plate inscriptions. Further copper plate records from King Madhavaraja I of Kangoda suggest that Kalinga remained under Sailodbhava rule. The Somavamsi rulers, credited with constructing the Barahi temple near Konark in the 9th century, also exerted influence in the region. However, it was Eastern Ganga King Narasimha Deva I who, in the 13th century, cemented Konark's historical significance by constructing the Sun Temple, a masterpiece of Indian architecture.

Analyzing various historical sources, it is evident that the Konark region was under the supervision of the Kalinga rulers. The genealogy of Kalinga's ruling lineage traces back to the Mahameghavahana dynasty.

Mahameghavahana Dynasty

The Mahameghavahana dynasty was a powerful ruling family in ancient Kalinga (present-day Odisha), with its most prominent ruler being Kharavela. Emerging in the 2nd century BCE, the dynasty played a crucial role in reviving Kalinga's power after its subjugation by the Mauryan Empire under Ashoka.

Kharavela, the most celebrated ruler of the dynasty, is renowned for his military campaigns, administrative efficiency, and patronage of Jainism. His Hathigumpha inscription, found in the Udayagiri caves near Bhubaneswar, provides detailed accounts of his conquests, infrastructure projects, and religious tolerance. He is credited with restoring Kalinga's independence, expanding its territory, and fostering trade and culture.

The dynasty significantly contributed to the region's economic prosperity and artistic development, particularly in rock-cut architecture. However, after Kharavela's reign, the Mahameghavahana dynasty gradually declined, paving the way for the rise of new regional powers.

Eastern Ganga Dynasty

The Eastern Ganga dynasty ruled Kalinga from the 5th century CE to the 15th century CE, leaving an enduring legacy in architecture, administration, and culture. One of its most notable rulers, Anantavarman Chodaganga Deva (1077–1147 CE) initiated the construction of the famous Jagannath Temple in Puri. The Eastern Gangas were great patrons of art and literature, ushering in a golden age in Odisha's history.

The dynasty also played a crucial role in resisting

Muslim invasions, particularly under Narasimha Deva I (1238–1264 CE), who is credited with constructing the iconic Konark Sun Temple. His military campaigns successfully repelled invasions from the Delhi Sultanate, preserving Kalinga's cultural and political identity.

The Eastern Ganga dynasty eventually declined in the 15th century, allowing the Gajapati dynasty to take control of Odisha. However, its architectural and cultural contributions remain significant, as seen in the temples and inscriptions that continue to define Odisha's historical landscape. Legends and archaeological findings indicate that the region later came under the rule of the Gajapati dynasty, followed by Muslim rulers and the Marathas. The presence of a Muslim tomb at Manikapatna further attests to this period of transition.

Revival and Influence of the Chalukyas and Cholas

After the decline of early Eastern Ganga rule, the Chalukyas of Vengi took control of the region. The first monarch of this revived dynasty, Vajrahastha Aniyakabhima I (980–1015 CE), took advantage of internal strife to reestablish Ganga power. During their rule, Shaivism gained prominence over Buddhism and Jainism. The magnificent Srimukhalingam Temple at Mukhalingam was constructed during this period.

In the 11th century, the Cholas brought the Ganga kingdom under their rule following the sudden death of DevendravarmanRajaraja I. His son, Anantavarman Chodaganga Deva, ascended the throne at the age of five under the protection of his maternal uncle from the Chola family. Despite multiple challenges, he successfully consolidated Kalinga, Vengi, Utkala, Odra, and parts of Bengal, uniting them into a single kingdom.

Later Eastern Ganga Rulers and Decline

Rajaraja III ascended the throne in 1198 CE but failed to resist the Ghurid Muslim invaders of the Khalji dynasty of Bengal, who attacked Odisha in 1206 CE. However, his son, AnangabhimaIII, successfully repelled these invasions and constructed the Megheswara Temple in Bhubaneswar.

Narasimhadeva I, son of Anangabhima III, invaded southern Bengal in 1243 CE, defeated the Delhi Sultanate's Muslim rulers, and captured Gauda, the capital. To commemorate this victory, he built the iconic Sun Temple at Konark. Narasimhadeva I was the first ruler to adopt the title "Gajapati" (Lord of War Elephants) in 1246 CE, as recorded in the Kapilash Temple inscription.

Following Narasimhadeva I's death in 1264 CE, the dynasty began to decline. The Delhi Sultan, Firuz Shah Tughlaq, invaded Odisha between 1353 and 1358 CE, imposing a tribute on the Ganga rulers. In 1356 CE, the MusunuriNayaks reportedly defeated the Ganga forces. The last known ruler, Narasimha IV, ruled until 1425 CE. His successor, Bhanudeva IV, known as the "mad king," left no inscriptions. His minister, Kapilendra Deva, overthrew him and established the Suryavamsha Dynasty in 1434–35 CE.

List of Eastern Ganga Rulers
Kalinga Rulers (c. 498 – 1077 CE)
1. Mittavarman (c. ??–498 CE) – Feudal under Vakataka rule
2. Indravarman I (c. 498–537 CE) – Founder of the dynasty

3. Samantavarman (c. 537–562 CE)
4. Hastivarman (c. 562–578 CE)
5. Indravarman II (c. 578–589 CE)
6. Danarnava (c. 589–652 CE)
7. Indravarman III (c. 652–682 CE)
8. Gunarnava (c. 682–730 CE)
9. Devendravarman I (c. 730–780 CE)
10. Anantavarman III (c. 780–812 CE)
11. Rajendravarman II (c. 812–840 CE)
12. Devendravarman V (c. 840–895 CE)
13. Gunamaharnava I (c. 895–910 CE)
14. Vajrahasta II (Anangabhimadeva I) (c. 910–939 CE)
15. Gundama I (c. 939–942 CE)
16. Kamarnava I (c. 942–977 CE)
17. Vinayaditya (c. 977–980 CE)
18. Vajrahasta IV (c. 980–1015 CE)
19. Kamarnava II (c. 1015 CE, ruled for 6 months)
20. Gundama II (c. 1015–1018 CE)
21. Madhukamarnava (c. 1018–1038 CE)
22. Vajrahasta V (c. 1038–1070 CE)
23. Rajaraja Deva I (c. 1070–1077 CE)

Trikalinga Rulers (c. 1077 – 1434 CE)

After the decline of early Eastern Ganga rule, the Chalukyas of Vengi took control of the region. The first monarch of this revived dynasty, VajrahasthaAniyakabhima I (980–1015 CE), took advantage of internal strife to re-establish Ganga power. During their rule, Shaivism gained prominence over Buddhism and Jainism. The magnificent Srimukhalingam Temple at Mukhalingam was constructed during this period.

In the 11th century, the Cholas brought the Ganga kingdom under their rule following the sudden death of DevendravarmanRajaraja I. His son, AnantavarmanChodaganga Deva, ascended the throne at the age of five under the protection of his maternal uncle from the Chola family. Despite multiple challenges, he successfully consolidated Kalinga, Vengi, Utkala, Odra, and parts of Bengal, uniting them into a single kingdom.

Intermarriage and the Formation of the Chodaganga Dynasty

The Eastern Gangas were known to have intermarried with the Cholas and Chalukyas, strengthening their political alliances. While the dynasty likely originated in the early 5th century CE, it became known as the Chodaganga dynasty towards the end of the 11th century, named after Anantavarman Chodaganga Deva.

Anantavarman was the son of Rajaraja Deva, ruler of Kalinga, and Rajasundari, a Chola princess and daughter of VirarajendraChola. He expanded his rule from the Ganges River in the north to the Godavari River in the south, firmly establishing the Eastern Ganga Dynasty. During his reign, he initiated the construction of the great Jagannath Temple at Puri. In 1076 CE, he assumed the title Trikalingadhipati (Ruler of the Three Kalingas—Kalinga proper, Utkala in the north, and Koshala in the west), making him the first to govern all three regions.

A devout patron of art and literature, Anantavarman was succeeded by a long line of distinguished rulers, including Narasimha Deva I (1238–1264 CE)).

Development of the Sun Temple

The Sun Temple at Konark is a grand 13th-century CE temple located in Konark, Odisha, India. It is widely believed to have been commissioned by King Narasimhadeva I of the Eastern Ganga Dynasty in 1255 CE. The temple is designed in the shape of a colossal chariot, adorned with 24 intricately carved stone wheels, numerous pillars, and elaborately decorated walls. Today, much of the temple lies in ruins, yet it remains an architectural marvel. Recognized as a UNESCO World Heritage Site, the Konark Sun Temple is also listed among the Seven Wonders of India. It stands approximately 35 kms from the renowned religious centre of Puri and 65 km from Bhubaneswar, the capital of Odisha.

The older Sun Temple within the Konark temple complex is smaller and follows the Saptaratha plan, whereas the massive Konark temple adheres to the Pancha Ratha plan. The AnurthaPaga of this temple is notably thinner than the other two pilasters. After carving, this Paga is barely visible, contributing to the temple's Pancha Ratha structure. This suggests that architects continued experimenting with Paga formation. Unlike later temples, which followed a perfect square plan, the Bimana and Jagamohana of the Konark Sun Temple are built on a rectangular plan. The sanctum and the interior of the Jagamohana are deeply recessed to align with the external pilaster arrangements. The open platform in front of the Jagamohana is elevated to the height of the temple's plinth, measuring three feet and three inches. The plinth is decorated with three belts—Khura, Kani, and Basanta—though the Bada of the platform lacks any mouldings.The inner walls of the temple are adorned with various murals, an uncommon feature in temples built beyond the 10th century. Talajangha exists just above the Pabhaga, though many vertical intersections associated with it have been lost over time. Parshwa Devatas are placed in niches on the south and north sides, while the western niche remains vacant. Above the Talajangha, the temple's Bandhan features five mouldings: Khura, Kumbha, Pata, Kani, and Basanta. While many of these mouldings have been lost, their arrangement indicates significant variation. The estimated height of this temple is moderate compared to other temples built between AD 700 and 1000.

The old Sun Temple predates the Konark Sun Temple by a few centuries. It was not constructed for Mayadevi or Chhaya Devi, as it is unlikely that a temple dedicated to the Sun God's consort would have been built centuries before the main Sun Temple at Konark[Altekar,1938].The construction of the Konark Sun Temple extensively utilized iron beams and Khondalite stone. The temple, shaped like a chariot, features 12 pairs of wheels, each with 8 wider and 8 inner spokes, totalling 24 in diameter. These 12 wheels symbolize the 12 months of the year, while the 8 spokes represent the 8 *praharas*(time divisions) of the day. Legend suggests that the temple functioned as a sundial, accurately determining the time of day based on the sun's position. The sundial was meticulously designed using complex mathematical calculations, considering the movements of the sun, moon, earth, and stars. It likely played a crucial role in religious ceremonies and rituals.

The temple's main entrance faces east, allowing the first rays of the sun to illuminate the idol of the Sun God inside the sanctuary. Various symbols depicting the sun's movement, akin to a clock, showcase the artisans' profound knowledge and skill. The architecture of the Konark Sun Temple reflects a society rich in culture, artistic talent, and advanced craftsmanship.This architectural marvel not only demonstrates artistic prowess but also signifies the political stability of the Eastern Ganga Dynasty during Narasimhadeva I's reign. Historical sources indicate his victory over the Maratha rulers, establishing a stable government capable of supporting large-scale temple construction through effective taxation.

The Konark Sun Temple stands as a testament to the cultural and artistic achievements of its time, influencing various art forms, including textile weaving and temple design. The temple was constructed to commemorate victory, greatness, and devotion to the Sun God. Despite the decline of many structures over time, its monumental size remains visible and is renowned for its exquisite carvings and decorations. The temple's sanctuary tower, once the tallest in the complex, collapsed in the 19th century due to structural and environmental factors. The temple's pyramidal roof covers the Jagamohana, or entrance hall. Due to the weight of the monumental structure and the region's weak soil, the tallest structure (Vimana) collapsed in 1837. The sanctuary tower was originally approximately twice as tall as the temple's current height[Kramrisch S,1938.].The concept of a chariot-form temple is not unique to Konark, though it remains the most splendid example of its kind. Ancient Indian manuscripts, such as the Puranas, mention three prominent sites of sun worship, with Konark originally known as Mandira. Later, it was renamed Konaditya or Konarka. The sanctity of the Sun Temple at Konark predates its present construction by Narasimhadeva I, as supported by texts like the Brahmapurana, which refers to a sun temple (Suryalayam) in this region.

The Sun Temple

The Sun Temple at Konark was built near the Chandrabhaga River, though the waterline has since receded. The temple resembles a giant ornamented chariot carrying the Sun God 'Surya' on twelve pairs of elaborately carved stone wheels, each about three meters wide and drawn by seven horses. The temple follows the traditional style of Kalinga architecture and is carefully oriented towards the east, allowing the first rays of sunrise to strike its main entrance. Most of the temple is constructed from Khondalite rocks. The principal sanctum sanctorum (Vimana) of the Sun Temple once stood approximately 229 feet (70 m) tall, but it collapsed in 1837 due to the structure's immense weight and the region's unique soil composition.

The Jagamohana, or audience hall, measures approximately 128 feet (39 meters) tall and remains the main surviving structure of the temple amidst its ruins. Other surviving structures include the roofless dance hall (Natamandira) and the dining hall (Bhogamandapa). The Sun Temple at Konark is also famous for its remarkable erotic sculptures.

Within the temple compound, two smaller ruined temples have been discovered southwest of the main structure. One is the Mayadevi Temple, dedicated to Mayadevi, one of the Sun God's wives, dating back to the 11th century. Another temple, dedicated to an unknown Vaishnava deity, features sculptures of Balarama, Varaha, and Trivikrama. Both temples have lost their primary idols, and fallen sculptures can be viewed at the Konark Archaeological Museum. Rabindranath Tagore described the Sun Temple at Konark as a place where "the language of stone surpasses the language of humans."

According to Hindu manuscripts like the BhavishyaPurana and Samba Purana, evidence suggests that a sun temple existed in the region as early as the 9th century, alongside temples in Mundira (Konark), Kalapriya (Mathura), and Multan. The exact cause of the collapse of the main sanctum remains uncertain, though it is believed that Kalapahad, who invaded Odisha in 1568, may have contributed to its destruction. In 1627, the Raja of Khurda reportedly removed the Sun idol from Konark to the Jagannath Temple in Puri.

The Sun Temple at Konark remains a stunning monument of religious significance and a masterpiece of Indian architecture. It exemplifies Odia architecture and is celebrated for its intricate stone carvings, symbolizing a monumental chariot carrying the Sun God. It also served as a crucial landmark for European sailors, earning it the nickname 'The Black Pagoda.'

References
- Behera, K. S. (1996). *Konarak: The heritage of mankind* (pp. 189–191). New Delhi, India: Aryan Books International.
- Mitra, R. L. (1875.). *The antiquities of Odisha* (Vol. 1, p. 93).
- O'Malley, L. S. S. (2007). *Bengal district gazetteer: Puri* (p. 283). New Delhi, India: Concept Publishing Company.

- Reddy, K. K. (2003). *Indian history* (p. 2). New Delhi, India: Tata McGraw-Hill Education.
- Stella Kramrisch. (1938). *The Hindu temple* (Vol. II, p. 306).
- Sun Temple. (1984). *Konarak*. UNESCO. Retrieved from https://whc.unesco.org/en/list/246/ (Include actual URL if available)
- Altekar, S. (1938). *Position of women in India* (p. 300).

Architectural Features and Layout

The temple—an orchestra carved in stone, designed with astronomical precision, and sculpted in the language of the cosmos—is none other than the Sun Temple at Konark. Set on the shores of Chandrabhaga, it stands as a timeless resonance of time, devotion, and celestial grandeur. This temple showcases the exquisite craftsmanship of Kalingan architecture. The Kalingan architecture refers to the distinct architectural style of ancient Odisha (historically known as Kalinga), primarily seen in temples built between the 6th and 15th centuries CE. This style is characterized by its unique structural elements, intricate carvings, and symbolic representation of Hindu cosmology. The *Ratha* (chariot) is a significant design element in Kalingan temple architecture. The temple plan is conceived as a massive stone chariot of the deity, symbolizing a celestial journey. The walls of the temple towers *(Shikhara)* are divided into vertical projections, creating a rhythmic pattern of recesses and projections. Tri-*Ratha* (Three Projections) – where the temple has three vertical projections: one in the centre and two at the sides. *Pancha-Ratha* (Five Projections) – where the temple wall has five divisions, creating a more intricate appearance. Example: Lingaraja Temple whereas Sapta-Ratha (Seven Projections) is a more complex temple design with seven projections and Nava-Ratha with nine projections.

The Sun Temple at Konark, a marvel sculpted in reverence to Surya, stands as a grand cosmic chariot drawn by seven majestic horses. Crafted in the *Saptaratha* (Seven-Ratha) style, the temple unfolds systematically from east to west, symbolizing the eternal journey of the sun across the sky. Each part of the complex is a symphony of sacred geometry and divine purpose. At its core lie distinct architectural segments, each holding a tale of devotion and craftsmanship in the sacred realm of *Kalingan* architecture, the temple is envisioned not merely as a structure but as a living, breathing human form—it's every contour infused with spiritual symbolism. Nowhere is this philosophy more vividly brought to life than in the majestic Sun Temple of Konark. The *Jagamohana*, rising to a regal 125 feet, stands as a monumental feat, while the *Vimana*, once towering at 229 feet6 inches, echoes in historical texts such as the *Madala Panji*. The width of the *Vimana*, spanning 81 feet 9 inches from *RahaPaga* to RahaPaga, and the Kalasha's impressive 25 feet height, as recorded by the Archaeological Survey of India (ASI), further emphasize the scale and elegance of this sun-dedicated sanctuary. Here, the Jagamohana's Bada unfolds with meticulous precision, divided into the elegant segments of Pabhaga, Talajangha, Bandhani, Uparajangha, and Baranda. The temple's architectural brilliance is further captured in its detailed elevation plans, a testament to the mastery of its creators. Horizontal banding—seen in the finely sculpted profiles of the Pabhaga, Jangha, Bandhani, and Baranda—adds rhythmic grace to the structure's vertical rise. Alas, time has not been kind to every crown of this marvel—all three Nisa Deulas (upper towers) have been lost to time. Yet, hope and heritage persevered, as restoration efforts in 1900 preserved two sets of detailed plans and elevations of the Jagamohana, allowing future generations to glimpse the grandeur that once was.

Beyond the central halls, the temple's sacred rhythm extends to its auxiliary structures, which whisper tales of ritual and celebration. All five temple units rest gracefully upon a common two-tiered plinth—the smaller *Padma Prustha* and the broader *Pratham Prustha* (also known as *Khura Prustha)*, forming the temple's sturdy base. Between the *Nata Mandira* and the *Jagamohana* lies the modest yet significant platforms, likely meant for musicians whose melodies once accompanied the ritual dances. These remnants affirm that music, like dance, was woven into the spiritual mosaic of *Konark,* elevating the temple into a multi-sensory celebration of divinity.

Thus, the Sun Temple of Konark is not just a marvel of stone—it is an embodiment of cosmic rhythm, human form, divine purpose, and artistic immortality, a legacy carefully preserved by the hands of time and the guardianship of the Archaeological Survey of India. **(www.asi.nic.in)**.

Konark is more than a temple—it is a gallery of life etched in stone, teeming with sculptures that celebrate art, dance, music, mythology, and human experience. The countless depictions of dancers across the temple walls reflect not only reflect artistic excellence but the belief that dance is life itself—a sacred expression of the soul's longing and joy. These sculptures, expressive in posture and poetic in detail, reveal that dance was not ornamental, but fundamental. It nurtured spiritual connection and social joy, thus leading to the thoughtful construction of the *Nata Mandira*—a space where architecture became performance and stone found rhythm. Nata Mandira (Dance Hall) at Konark is gracefully set apart from the main sanctuary; this space was not merely a stage but a living canvas where art merged with spirituality. It offered an ethereal platform for ritual dance and devotion, where the rhythm of Odissi once echoed in divine cadence. Tourists and pilgrims alike are captivated by the hall's elegance—it's very stones seem to sway with frozen movements of celestial dancers, immortalized in sculptural grace. As recorded and preserved by the Archaeological Survey of India (www.asi.nic.in), the Sun Temple at Konark remains one of India's most magnificent evidences to artistic vision, cosmic symbolism, and devotional grandeur.

Encasing this celestial monument is a mighty rectangular boundary wall, stretching approximately 261.2 meters by 164.6 meters, fashioned from the resilient and locally sourced khondalite stone. These stones, chosen for both their strength and beauty, lend a timeless grandeur to the edifice. The temple's strategic gateways—positioned on the eastern and southern flanks—once welcomed pilgrims into a sacred world where artistry and devotion converged.

Other Foundational Elements and Ritual Spaces

The architectural elegance of the Konark Sun Temple extends beyond its towering sanctum and halls, embracing a constellation of auxiliary structures that enrich its ceremonial and functional landscape. Among these are the Nyasa Mandapa, where the sacred Puja image was ritually consecrated; the Parayatra Mandapa, which served as a ceremonial hall for divine processions; and the Bajeni Mandapa, a platform that once resonated with the music of temple musicians. Complementing these are two Yupas or sacrificial pillars, symbolizing the temple's ritualistic depth and its connection to Vedic traditions. Each of these elements adds a distinct layer to the complex's sacred geography, showcasing the spiritual choreography that once unfolded within its walls.

Historical Records and Architectural Dimensions

Illuminating the temple's historic scale and royal patronage, the Madala Panji, Odisha's traditional chronicle, recounts how King Narsinghdeva-I—son of Prushottamdeva and grandson of Ramchandra deva of the Khurda dynasty—commissioned the temple's precise measurement. This task was entrusted to Swasia Natha Mohapatra during the period when Baqur Khan served as Subedar under Emperor Shah Jahan. Initially measured as 120 Kathi, the temple's dimensions were translated through traditional units such as Hata and Anguli into feet. However, ambiguities arose due to the exclusion of the *Mastaka*—the towering crowning structure—thus leaving a gap in the full spatial record.

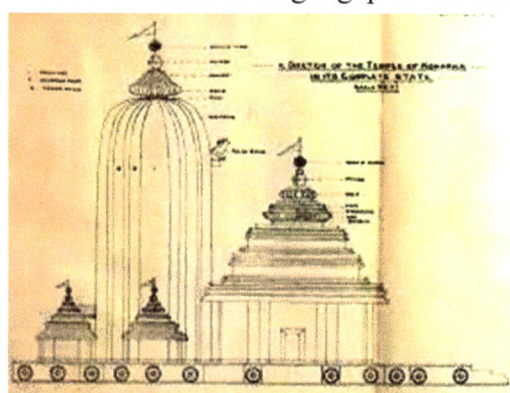

Sketch of the Temple in its complete state: (Swarup, Bahinipati, Biswal & Suar)

The Nata Mandap and Evolution of Form

One of the temple's most distinctive features is the *Nata mandapa,* or dance pavilion, which adopts a *Pancharatha* plan and rests on three elegantly tiered plinths. It bears testimony to the evolution of temple architecture in *Odisha,* blending ritualistic function with sculptural splendour. The inclusion of *Gajasimhas*—lion-elephant hybrid motifs—and intricately crafted staircases reflect not just aesthetic brilliance but also the highly considered spatial planning behind this ceremonial space.

Ritual Infrastructure and Sacred Logistics

The Konark Sun Temple is renowned not only for its grand architectural brilliance but also for its intricate sculptures and carvings, which vividly narrate both spiritual themes and worldly life. These carvings seamlessly blend art, mythology, and astronomical symbolism, showcasing the advanced craftsmanship and profound cosmological knowledge of its builders.

Beyond its spiritual symbolism, the temple was meticulously designed to support the rhythms of daily ritual life. Archaeological remains of a dedicated kitchen complex and allied structures point to a well-organized sacred infrastructure. Though now partially in ruins, these facilities suggest the elaborate scale of offerings, communal feasts, and festivals once conducted at the site. Such arrangements reflect a vibrant sacred economy, where divine worship was closely intertwined with the practicalities of human sustenance and social cohesion.

Sculptural Storytelling: Secular and Sacred

The temple's narrative is etched in stone, with its walls

and pillars bearing thousands of intricate sculptures that can broadly be classified into two categories:

Secular Sculptures: These vividly portray scenes from everyday life—musicians, dancers, hunters, lovers, and tradesmen—offering profound insights into the socio-economic and cultural fabric of 13th-century Odisha. They reflect the artistic consciousness, aspirations, and lived realities of the time.

Artistic Techniques and Craftsmanship

The use of khondalite stone enabled artisans to execute delicate details and intricate patterns with remarkable precision. Techniques refined over centuries are evident in the smooth contours, elaborate floral motifs, and geometric designs embellishing every surface of the temple. Each carving stands as a testament to the technical skill and artistic innovation of its creators.

Unlike standalone artworks, the sculptures at Konark are integrally woven into the fabric of the temple's architecture. Carvings appear on walls, pillars, doorways, and even the beams that support the structure. This seamless integration creates a continuous visual narrative that guides visitors through the temple complex. The play of light and shadow further accentuates these details at different times of the day.

The artistic expression evident in Konark's carvings has influenced generations of artisans and remains a cornerstone of Indian cultural heritage. These detailed sculptures not only record mythological and religious narratives but also encapsulate the aspirations, beliefs, and everyday experiences of the society that built them. Despite centuries of weathering and partial decay, the sculptures of Konark continue to inspire admiration for their beauty and ingenuity. They stand as a lasting reminder of the advanced knowledge of astronomy, mathematics, and art that prevailed during the temple's construction.

Building on the temple's impressive architectural framework, the sculptures further illuminate the cultural, social, and artistic milieu of 13th-century Odisha. These carvings enhance the monument's aesthetic appeal while serving as a dynamic record of the era's multifaceted life. Among the sculptures, the Mundis are particularly noteworthy. Carved in bas-relief directly into the temple walls, these miniature temples are classified into three distinct types:

Pidha Mundis: Resembling Pidha-style temples, typically found in the upper jangha (vertical wall section), their design echoes traditional temple forms and reinforces the sanctity of the space.

Khakara Mundis: With a form reminiscent of the southern Indian Gopuram, these adorn the lower jangha. Their distinctive silhouette reflects cross-cultural influences and highlights the region's architectural diversity.

Bajra Mundis: Combining features of medallions with Khakara design elements; these appear in both upper and lower janghas of the Nata Mandira (dance hall). This variety underscores mutual respect for cultural diversity and the exchange of regional artistic traditions (konark.nic.in).

Another significant motif is the Kirtimukha, a fierce, face-like figure derived from Buddhist Chaitya sculptures. Located in the Rahapaga of the Gandi portion, the Kirtimukha serves as a guardian symbol, embodying protective power over the sacred precinct. The temple's walls are also adorned with intricate carvings of trees, flowers, and scrollwork. These natural motifs embellish the surfaces while suggesting an early recognition of environmental harmony and sustainability, reflecting the societal importance of nature during that period.

The sculptures provide valuable insights into 13th-century attire and personal adornment. Women are depicted in a variety of sari styles, representing both royal elegance and everyday wear. Hairstyles range from simple combed-back looks to elaborate arrangements featuring pigtails and *juda*, often adorned with intricately woven flowers. Ornamentation such as earrings, bracelets, waistbands (like Kali *bandhan or Mekhala bandhan*), and anklets accentuate feminine grace. Men are typically shown wearing simple dhotis. Soldiers appear in short dhotis suitable for marching, accessorized with kerchiefs, caps, and sometimes footwear. These depictions convey not only fashion but also practical aspects of military life.

Beyond portraiture, the sculptures capture the essence of daily life and societal values. Numerous carvings depict musical instruments such as the veena, kahala, conch shell, and drums like the mardala or dholaki, highlighting music's significance in ceremonial and public life. Dance forms—solo, duet, group performances, Odissi, and martial arts dances (paika or chau)—reflect the vibrant performing arts traditions of the time. Scenes of teaching with disciples gathered around mentors, gestures of respect such as folded hands, and depictions of a woman touching another's feet emphasize reverence, familial bonds, and cultural transmission.

Carvings portraying cooking, hunting, and even vegetable cutting offer glimpses into domestic life. Agricultural activities—such as a man carrying a plough—alongside household furnishings like the stone-carved "Simhasana" (lion throne) illustrate the socio-economic foundations of the era. Maritime trade is subtly referenced through depictions of boats, while detailed ironwork highlights the region's metallurgical expertise. Dynamic panels depict military activities with elephant riders, infantry formations, and cavalry scenes, underscoring the strategic importance of warfare and military organization. Combined with trade and commerce depictions, these images paint a comprehensive picture of the region's economic and military strength.

The sculptures of Konark are seamlessly integrated into the temple's architecture, serving as both decorative and narrative elements. They chronicle a society that valued artistic expression, respected nature, and maintained strong familial and social bonds. These elaborate carvings celebrate religious devotion while documenting the cultural richness, daily practices, and economic activities of 13th-century Odisha.

Martanda Bhairav in a dancing pose on a boat.

By merging mythological symbolism with depictions of daily life, the sculptures create a vivid tapestry of history—one that continues to inspire admiration for its technical excellence and artistic innovation. Their intricate details stand as a testament to the ingenuity of the temple's creators and the enduring legacy of Odisha's culture.

Dedicated to Surya, the Sun God, revered in Hindu mythology as both creator and sustained of life, the temple's design is deeply symbolic. Its structure mimics a colossal chariot inspired by the legendary tale of Balram—elder brother of Lord Krishna—driving the Sun God's chariot.

This mythological connection enriches the temple's religious allure and cements its status as a revered pilgrimage site for devotees across India.

The temple is celebrated for its awe-inspiring and scientifically advanced design. Functioning as a colossal sundial, its intricately carved wheels were engineered to mark time accurately throughout the day. The deliberate east-west alignment ensures that the first rays of the rising sun penetrate the main entrance, illuminating the sanctum. This design reflects the ancient architects' profound understanding of celestial movements and solar symbolism, blending art with astronomical precision.

Although the main sanctum (sanctum sanctorum) is no longer accessible, daily rituals continue at an external altar where water offerings and Vedic chants are performed, highlighting the temple's enduring spiritual significance. Recognized as one of the four Dhams in Hinduism, the Sun Temple serves as a source of blessings for devotees seeking health, prosperity, and resolution of personal troubles.

The cultural vibrancy of Konark is further exemplified through its annual religious festivals. Notably, during the RathYatra, a grand procession carries a statue of Suryadev on a chariot, attracting devotees from far and wide. This celebration reaffirms the temple's religious importance and its role as a cultural hub where ancient traditions continue to thrive.

In essence, the Sun Temple of *Konark* is far more than an architectural marvel; it is a cultural and scientific treasure that encapsulates the ancient Indian civilization's deep reverence for the Sun God and its advanced understanding of astronomy and timekeeping. Its enduring legacy of spiritual devotion, combined with its artistic and technical brilliance, continues to inspire awe and reverence among visitors and worshipers alike.

Religious Sculptures

Deeply symbolic and profoundly devotional, the temple's religious carvings breathe life into mythological tales and spiritual allegories, firmly establishing the sanctuary as a gateway to the divine. The walls and pillars are adorned with exquisitely chiselled images of deities, celestial beings, and mythological figures, chief among them Surya, the Sun God. His majestic form graces numerous panels, eloquently conveying both his immense power and benevolent presence. Alongside Surya, a pantheon of gods, goddesses, and demigods occupy niches and friezes, weaving timeless narratives drawn from Hindu mythology and reinforcing the temple's sacred purpose. Many of these religious sculptures are meticulously positioned to engage with the sun's rays; their arrangement aligns with the daily path of the sun, thereby contributing to the temple's function as a monumental sundial. This celestial synchronization epitomizes the seamless fusion of art and science that flourished in medieval Indian culture.

Beyond its religious iconography, the temple also boasts an abundant collection of secular carvings that offer invaluable insights into the social and cultural fabric of 13th-century Odisha. Intricately detailed panels depict scenes from courtly life, musical performances, dance rituals, and everyday activities, providing a vivid window into the era's socio-economic realities and refined aesthetic sensibilities.

Among the most striking features of the Konark

sculptures is the presence of erotic imagery. Far from mere ornamentation, these bold and intricate representations symbolize fertility, prosperity, and the eternal cycles of creation and rebirth. They eloquently reflect a culture that embraced the sacred and the sensual as interwoven dimensions of existence, celebrating life's fullness in all its facets.

Stories and Legends Associated with the Temple

The legends surrounding the Konark Sun Temple are steeped in mythology and historical significance, intertwining religious fervour with extraordinary tales of human endeavour and divine intervention

Sacred Origins and Mythical Foundations

According to tradition, King Narasimhadeva-I chose the site of Konark not only for its strategic advantages but also for its profound sanctity. Numerous ancient manuscripts—including the *KapilaSamhita*, *MadalaPanji*, and *PrachiMahatmya*—trace the temple's sanctity back to mythical times, drawing on earlier traditions found in the *BhavisyaPurana* and the *Samba Purana*. These texts underscore that the temple's spiritual significance predates its current structure, embedding it deeply in the lore of sun worship.

Alternate Construction Legend Involving Divine Intervention

Another legend recounts an unusual incident during the temple's construction. It is said that a stone dropped by King Narasimha Deva near a pool which was swiftly swallowed by a Raghab Fish, an event that disrupted the goddess Dhama. In response, she advised Sivai Santara to initiate a construction method by dropping stones from the sides, leading to the creation of the temple through divine guidance.

The Story of Dharmapada (Dharama)

A poignant tale from the 13th century tells of the immense human effort behind the temple's construction. Approximately 1,200 workers laboured for 12 years to build the temple across a sprawling 12-acre site during the reign of King Narasimhadeva I. Designed in the form of a celestial chariot, the structure was an engineering masterpiece, held together with interlocked metals and even two massive magnets weighing more than five tonnes. It is said that the idol of the Sun God was crafted from an alloy of eight metals and suspended mid-air, balanced by these powerful magnets.

Under a strict deadline, King Narasimhadeva I threatened to behead the workers if the temple was not completed on time. Although the structure was finished, the crown stone could not be fixed. The chief architect, overwhelmed by despair, sank into depression. In this dire moment, a 12-year-old boy named Dharmapada approached him, offering a solution to fix the crown stone. Revealing that he was the long-lost son of the chief architect, Dharmapada resolved the mounting problem. However, fearing that the king might later punish the workers for relying on a child's ingenuity, Dharmapada tragically leaped from the temple into the Chandrabhaga River. His suicide rendered the temple unholy, and it is said that the Sun God was never worshipped there in the same manner.

Spiritual and Cultural Legacy

These legends not only highlight the spiritual significance and divine origins of the Konark Sun Temple but also underscore its rich cultural heritage and intricate ties to Hindu mythology. Over the centuries, the temple has continued to attract both pilgrims and tourists. Its sacred location is celebrated during festivals such as Magha Sukla Saptami (also known as Chandrabhaga Yatra), when thousands of devotees bathe in the Chandrabhaga River, witness the sunrise from the beach, and offer worship to the Navagrahas within the complex.

The Curse of Konark Temple

A legend claims that the Konark Temple was cursed, leading to its decline. It is said that King Narasimhadeva I sought to establish the temple as the most magnificent shrine dedicated to Surya. However, some believe that its construction angered the gods, resulting in its eventual abandonment and destruction. Others suggest that the temple was never meant to be completed, attributing its downfall to the forces of nature, divine intervention, or even dark energy. While this story lacks historical verification, it adds to the mystery surrounding why the temple remains incomplete in certain aspects.

The Magnetic Power of Konark

Some ancient texts and folk stories mention that the Konark Sun Temple once had a powerful magnet in its central dome. The magnet was so strong that it allegedly disrupted the compasses of ships passing through the Bay of Bengal. Some believe that iron rods within the temple created a magnetic force, making the idol of Surya appear to float in mid-air. According to legend, the British removed this magnet to protect their ships, which ultimately contributed to the temple's gradual collapse While this story lacks scientific proof, it remains a fascinating part of Konark's folklore.

Scholarly Interpretations and the Chandrabhaga River Debate

The temple's proximity to the Chandrabhaga River is itself a subject of legend and scholarly debate. While many ancient texts—such as the *SkandaPurana*, *PrachiMahatmya*, *BhavishyaPurana*, *Samba Purana*, *KapilaSamhita*, *MadalaPanji*, and the *Sarala Mahabharata*—affirm the river's historical presence near Konark, interpretations vary among scholars;

Pandit Krupasindhu Mishra argues that Konark was once situated at the river's mouth and that the deep Maitreya Vana eventually evolved over 4,000 years into the present-day town of Konark. He cites Golara Village, once a forested area with a medieval fort, as evidence of this transformation.

Engineer Bishan Swarup, who led the 19th-century restoration of the temple, maintained that the Chandrabhaga River did not flow near Konark; he suggested instead that the Chenab (Chandrabhaga) belonged to Punjab—the same river associated with Samba's legend of the Mitravana Sun Temple.

Professor Karuna Sagar Behera supports the notion found in the *Samba Purana*, which recounts Samba's construction of a sun temple on the banks of the Chandrabhaga (Chenab) River in Punjab. He proposes that the original Mitravana Sun Temple may have been near the sea, akin to today's Balukhand forest reserve that stretches from Konark to Puri.

Modern scientific investigations using remote sensing, satellite imagery, ground-penetrating radar, and GIS techniques by researchers from IIT Kharagpur suggest that, as recently as around 1919, the Chandrabhaga River did indeed flow beside the temple. These findings lend weight to the traditional accounts and literary sources, reinforcing the river's historical significance in the temple's myths.

References

- Archaeological Museum, Konarak; Archaeological Survey of India. (n.d.). *World Heritage Sites: Konarak Sun Temple*. Retrieved from http://www.asi.nic.in
- Archaeological Survey of India. (n.d.). *Konarak Sun Temple: Mithuna Sculptures*. Retrieved from http://www.asi.nic.in
- Archaeological Survey of India. (n.d.). *Konarak, conservation*. Retrieved from http://www.asi.nic.in
- Chary, M. T. (2009, February 2). *India: Nation on the move: An overview of India's people, culture, history, economy, IT industry, & more* (p. 389). I Universe.
- Chenna, N. K. (2009). *Textbook of engineering geology* (p. 188). Macmillan Publishers India Limited.
- Cunningham, S. A. (1871). *The ancient geography of India: I. The Buddhist period, including the campaigns of Alexander, and the travels of Hwen-Thsang* (p. 233). London, England: Trübner & Company.
- Davidson, L. K., & Gitlitz, D. M. (2002, January 1).

- *Pilgrimage: From the Ganges to Graceland: An encyclopedia* (p. 318). California, USA: ABC-CLIO.
- Description from British Library. (2009, March 26). Retrieved from http://www.bl.uk/onlinegallery/onlineex/apac
- Kelley, D. H., &Milone, E. F. (2011, February 16). *Exploring ancient skies: A survey of ancient and cultural astronomy.* Springer.
- Mayarani, P. (2015, December). Astronomical heritage: The Sun Temple-Konark. *Journal of the Indian Institute of Architects, 80*(12), 17.
- Mitra, R. L. (n.d.). *The antiquities of Odisha* (Vol. 1, p. 93).
- N. K. Singh. (2009). *Coronation of Shiva: Rediscovering Masrur Temple* (p. 18). New Delhi, India: Har-Anand Publications Pvt. Limited.
- O'Malley, L. S. S. (2007). *Bengal district gazetteer: Puri* (p. 283). New Delhi, India: Concept Publishing Company.
- Reddy, K. K. (2003). *Indian history* (p. 2). New Delhi, India: Tata McGraw-Hill Education.
- Rosenfield, J. M. (1967, January 1). *The dynastic arts of the Kushans* (p. 195). California, USA: University of California.
- Selin, H. (2008, April 16). *Encyclopedia of the history of science, technology, and medicine in non-Western cultures* (p. 1731). Berlin, Germany: Springer.
- Sen, S. (2013). *A textbook of medieval Indian history* (pp. 121–122). New Delhi, India: Primus Books.
- Sengupta, S. (2012, September 22). Poetry in stone. *Daily Pioneer.*
- Stella Kramrisch. (1937). *The Hindu temple* (Vol. II, p. 306).
- Sun Temple. (n.d.). *Konârak.* UNESCO. Retrieved from https://whc.unesco.org/en/list/246/

- The Sun Temple. (2017). *Tourism Department, Government of Orissa*. Retrieved May 20, 2017, from http://www.konark.nic.in
- Tourism Department, Government of Orissa. (n.d.). *The Sun Temple Legend*. Retrieved from http://www.konark.org/legend-konark.html
- Travelogue. (2011, July 7). *Konark Sun Temple*. Retrieved from http://www.premaanand-travelogue.blogspot.in/2011/07/konark-sun-temple-puri-orissa-india.html
- Varghese, P. C. (2012, November). *Engineering geology for civil engineers* (p. 126). PHI Learning Pvt. Ltd.

Where the Stones Speak- Sculptural Treasures of Konark

Sacred Stone: The Distinctive Statues of Konark
Konark is not only celebrated for its monumental Sun Temple but also for the extraordinary array of sculptural masterpieces that adorn it. These rare statues, carved with unmatched finesse, depict deities, celestial beings, mythical creatures, and scenes from daily life. Each figure is a fragment of a grand stone chronicle—an artistic dialogue between divinity, nature, and humanity. From the graceful dancers frozen in eternal rhythm to the majestic lions and elephants guarding the sanctum, these sculptures embody the spirit of 13th-century Odisha, where art and devotion met in perfect harmony.

Makara: The Mythical Aquatic Guardian in Indian and Odishan Art
In the vast lexicon of Indian mythological symbolism, few motifs are as enduring and evocative as the *makara*—a fantastic composite creature that merges the terrestrial with the aquatic, the real with the imagined. In Indian and especially Odishan art, the makara is not merely a decorative form but a deeply potent emblem. Traditionally

depicted with the head of an elephant or a crocodile and the body of a fish or other aquatic animal, the makara is a complex icon, intimately associated with water, fertility, and auspiciousness.

The makara's presence across Indian temple architecture, sculpture, and traditional jewellery speaks volumes about its symbolic power and adaptability. A mythical, crocodile-like creature linked to the primordial Waters of Creation, the makara is more than ornamental—it is cosmological. In architectural contexts, particularly in Odisha, the makara often denotes the presence of water, appearing prominently on temple pillars, gateways, and even as *gargoyle-like* waterspouts, where it channels the life-giving force of water with grace and ferocity.

The architectural expression of the makara in Odisha is especially vivid. As an auspicious symbol of Water Cosmology, it is a perennially favoured motif—frequently incorporated into the capital sections of pillars, projecting majestically above the shaft. It is also found on archways and niches, often as a part of the exquisitely carved *Makara Torana*—decorative arches typically framing doorways. A striking example of such a motif can be seen at the torana of the iconic 10th-century *Muktesvara Temple* in Bhubaneswar, where the makara heads at the base of the arch support a dynamic narrative of protection, fecundity, and divine order.

In the present images, photographed by Saroj Kumar Mohapatra at the 13th-century *Sun Temple of Konark*, the makara is shown as a dynamic creature brimming with energy. It supports itself on two forepaws, its mouth agape to reveal rows of sharp teeth and a distinctive double tongue. Lotus blossoms dangle from its lower jaw, while frothy dribbles spill from its flanks, emphasizing its aquatic origin. Its raised, curved snout and bulging, circular eyes lend it an alert, almost sentient presence. A delicately scrolled ornament crowns its forehead, completing the creature's regal yet fierce countenance.

Dr. Ramesh Prasad Mohapatra, one of India's most eminent archaeologists and art historians, has offered comprehensive insights into the makara motif in his works such as *Fashion Styles of Ancient India* (1992), *Archaeology in Orissa* (1986), and *Ornaments of Orissa* (1998, co-authored with Dr. Thomas E. Donaldson). He notes the transregional journey of this motif, observing how it travelled beyond Indian shores to influence art in Southeast Asia. In particular, the *Kalamakara* ornament found in Javanese sculpture bears striking resemblance to the makara figures seen at the base of arches and the *kirttimukha* faces that crown Odishan architectural ensembles.

While the makara is predominantly associated with water and aquatic realms, it is also closely linked to fertility, virility, and strength. In iconographic contexts, it is often depicted in the company of deities like Lakshmi—the goddess of wealth and abundance—or Kama, the god of love and desire. In jewellery traditions too, the makara appears frequently, particularly in bangles, armlets, and pendants, where it symbolizes prosperity, good fortune, and protection. According to *Jewels of India*, the use of the makara in ornamentation reinforces its auspicious associations, making it a cherished motif in both sacred and secular art.

In juxtaposition, another related motif—the *kirttimukha*, often found alongside the makara on temple walls and gateways—represents a fierce, protective face rooted in Hindu mythology. While the kirttimukha embodies the power of sacrifice and self-destruction in service of the divine, the makara channels the elemental strength of nature, especially water, as a source of life, mystery, and renewal. In essence, the makara is not just a decorative element—it is a symbolic threshold between the known and the unknown, the material and the metaphysical. Its continued presence across centuries of Indian and Odishan art reflects its enduring relevance as a guardian, nurturer, and carrier of cultural memory.

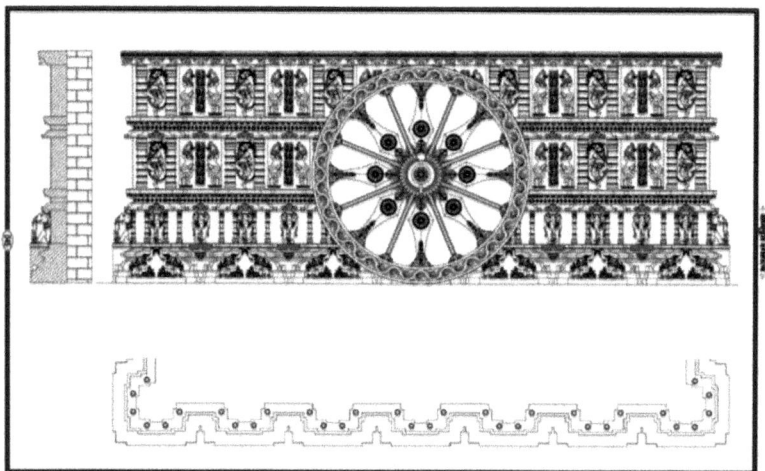

Dance and Music in Ancient Odisha: An Eternal Legacy Etched in Stone

The historical roots of dance and music in Odisha trace back to ancient times, as evidenced by archaeological findings in caves and temple carvings. One of the earliest known references comes from the *Manchapuri cave* in Udayagiri, where intricate carvings of dancers and musicians are dated to the reign of Jain King Kharavela (1st–2nd century BCE). These are among the earliest visual depictions of performative arts in India.

As temple architecture flourished in Odisha between the 10th to 14th centuries CE, so too did the representation of dance and music in sculptural form. Temples dedicated to various traditions—Vaishnavism, Shaivism, Shaktism, and the worship of Surya—carry exquisite carvings that vividly depict Odissi dance poses, musicians with traditional instruments, and joyous festival scenes. The Jagannath Temple in Puri, the Brahmeswara Temple in Bhubaneswar, and most magnificently, the Konark Sun Temple, preserve these expressions in sculpted stone, serving as enduring testaments to the centrality of dance and music in Odia culture and spirituality.

Motifs of Dance and Music in the Sculptures of Konark Sun Temple

The 13th-century Sun Temple at Konark, built by King Narasimha Deva I, is perhaps the most celebrated canvas of Odishan sculptural art. A UNESCO World Heritage Site, Konark is renowned for its architectural grandeur as well as its rich visual narrative of dance and music.Scattered across the temple walls, pillars, and wheel spokes are hundreds of intricately carved figures of dancers in dynamic Odissi poses, musicians with instruments like the mardala, veena, flute, and cymbals, and divine ensembles evoking celestial performances. These motifs do not merely decorate the temple—they celebrate the union of the arts with the divine, embodying the spirit of *Natya Shastra* and *Bhakti Rasa*.

Notable sculptural motifs at Konark include:
- Female dancers in tribhangi poses, with expressive hand gestures (*mudras*) and rhythmic movement frozen in stone.

- Musicians playing the mardala (percussion instrument)—an important accompaniment in classical Odissi dance.
- Couples engaged in coordinated dance, highlighting the social and festive nature of music and movement.
- Celestial beings (gandharvas and apsaras) performing amidst floral scrolls and mythical motifs.
- The massive wheels of the chariot, with spokes often adorned by miniature dancers and musicians.

These carvings not only demonstrate technical mastery but also provide a visual documentation of the instruments, costumes, and dance forms prevalent in medieval Odisha.

Rare Sculptural Panels:
1. Veena Player with a Dancer – On the outer walls of the Natya Mandapa, a panel shows a veena player seated in rapt attention as a female dancer performs.
2. Mardala and Cymbals Ensemble – Found near the base of one of the temple walls, a group of three musicians,

all women, are seen playing different instruments.
3. Wheel Spoke Dancer Reliefs – Miniature dancers carved delicately into the spokes of the colossal stone wheels, showcasing their iconic stance.
4. Gandharva Panel – A celestial figure with wings playing a flute amid floral motifs, symbolizing the divine connection of music.
5. Apsara in Motion – A dynamic sculpture of an apsara mid-dance, her anklets and ornaments carved with fine detailing, suggesting movement and grace.
Bottom of Form

Source: Markus Lerner- Musicians and Dancers

Animal Sculptures

Beyond its wealth of mythological, human, semi-divine, and divine imagery, the Konark Sun Temple complex also abounds with exquisite depictions of birds and animals, each rendered with symbolic depth and architectural ingenuity. The crocodile motif on the Chhayadevi/Mayadevi Temple serves a dual purpose: it is not only a remarkable piece of sculptural art but also a *pranala* or drainage spout, designed to channel out the consecrated water used during the deity's ritual bath (*abhisheka*). The lifelike detailing of the crocodile reflects the artisans' keen observation of nature, while its role as a water outlet symbolizes the temple's seamless fusion of aesthetic beauty, ritual significance, and practical design.

The sculpture of the giraffe at the Konark Sun Temple is among its most intriguing and rare depictions. Carved on the temple walls, it stands as a remarkable testament to the far-reaching maritime and trade connections of medieval Odisha. Since giraffes are not native to India, their presence in Konark's carvings suggests contact with African regions through sea routes. The artisans, with keen observation and imaginative skill, captured the animal's elongated neck and graceful form with astonishing accuracy. This exotic motif reflects the global awareness, artistic curiosity, and cosmopolitan vision of the builders of Konark.

Lost Grandeur

The original Konark Sun Temple was a magnificent architectural marvel, a grand chariot of the Sun God carved in stone, once comprising several imposing structures. Today, only the Jagamohana (audience hall) survives in its near entirety, while the towering Deul (sanctum), the Natya Mandir (dance hall), and the Bhoga Mandap (offering hall) have long since succumbed to time. The now-lost Deul, which once crowned the sanctum sanctorum, is believed to have mirrored the architectural style of the Jagannath Temple in Puri, both in form and grandeur. Built from dark chlorite stone, the temple earned the name "Black Pagoda" from early European sailors who used it as a navigational landmark along the eastern coast of India.

According to historical and archaeological estimates, the vimana (tower) of the Deul once soared to an awe-inspiring height of 229 feet (70 meters)—a testament to the engineering brilliance and artistic vision of the 13th-century Ganga dynasty.

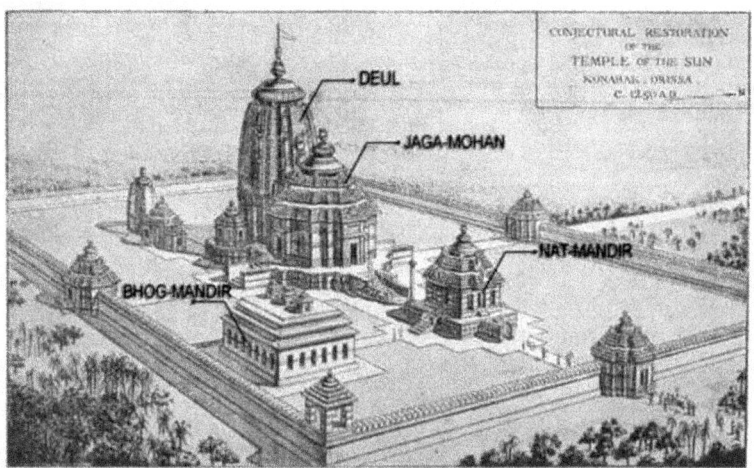

Sketch of the KT in its complete state (Swarup, 1910).

Reclaiming the Sacred Feminine: A Feminist Reinterpretation of Konark's Erotic Sculptures

The erotic sculptures of the Konark Sun Temple, often misinterpreted as mere expressions of sensuality, reveal a profound celebration of sacred feminine power, autonomy, and equality when viewed through a modern feminist lens. Rather than passive objects of male desire, the women depicted in these carvings are active participants in cosmic creation, reflecting the Tantric tradition's reverence for sexuality as a spiritual force. This interpretation reframes the sculptures as symbols of empowerment that challenge patriarchal narratives by portraying gender roles in balance, where both men and women engage equally in acts of divine creation. Unlike modern depictions of eroticism shaped by the male gaze and commercialization, the Konark figures celebrate the female body as a source of spiritual strength and liberation. Their placement on a sacred monument affirms sexuality as an integral part of the divine, inviting contemporary feminist movements to reclaim these images as expressions of female agency and cosmic harmony. By bridging ancient symbolism with present-day ideals, the reinterpretation of Konark's art fosters a deeper, more inclusive dialogue on gender, spirituality, and empowerment.

Source: Saroj Kumar Mahapatra

Far from being mere representations of sensuality, these sculptures embody deep philosophical, spiritual, and symbolic meanings rooted in India's tantric, aesthetic, and metaphysical traditions.

Konark, like many medieval temples of Odisha, flourished during a period of strong Tantric influence. Tantra perceives the universe as the interplay of Shiva (consciousness) and Shakti (energy). The erotic union on temple walls symbolizes the cosmic union of Purusha and Prakriti—the dynamic principle of creation itself. Thus, the imagery celebrates the divine energy that sustains the universe, not carnal pleasure.

The sculptures also signify the comprehensive sport of the world (Lila or Sanasar), in which every form of life, from the sacred to the sensual, is a manifestation of the Divine. By including erotic scenes alongside celestial beings, dancers, musicians, and mythical creatures, the temple portrays the totality of existence—the world in its most complete form revolving around the Sun, the eternal source of life.

Another school of thought interprets these sculptures as symbolic of the journey from desire to detachment. The devotee entering the temple first encounters the outer walls adorned with erotic imagery—representing the world of senses and passions. As one moves inward toward the sanctum, the art becomes more spiritual, suggesting that one must transcend worldly desires to reach the Divine core—the Surya or ultimate truth within.

From an artistic standpoint, the presence of erotic art celebrates life-affirmation and fertility, crucial to the agrarian societies that worshipped the Sun as the life-giver. Psychologically, it may serve as a cathartic representation of human instincts, allowing sublimation through sacred visualization rather than suppression. Folk and ritualistic traditions in medieval Odisha also associated such sculptures with apotropaic purposes—believing that the depiction of sexual imagery could ward off evil spirits, lightning, and natural calamities. This belief stemmed from the idea that the gods of destruction and nature would be distracted or appeased by these forms.

Some interpretations suggest that the erotic panels were meant to test the spiritual maturity of devotees. Only those who could look beyond sensual distractions and perceive the deeper symbolism were deemed ready to approach the sanctum—the realm of inner illumination. The sculptures at Konark epitomize the Indian philosophical conviction that no aspect of life is outside the domain of the sacred. The divine manifests equally in the ascetic and the sensual, the celestial and the earthly. This holistic worldview is central to Indian aesthetics, where beauty, desire, and devotion intertwine seamlessly.

In essence, the erotic sculptures of Konark represent a multilayered dialogue between art, philosophy, and spirituality. They are not expressions of indulgence but affirmations of a civilization that embraced the totality of existence—seeing the sensual and the spiritual as complementary paths toward the same eternal truth.

The Tantrik Rituals at Konark

The Konark Sun Temple is often celebrated for its stunning erotic sculptures, mythological tableaux, and vibrant depictions of dance and music. Yet, to view Konark through only these lenses is to miss its deeper social and cultural layers. The temple is also a mirror to the diverse and complex spiritual practices of ancient India. One such intriguing glimpse is found in a sculpture believed to represent the rituals of the Kapalika sect, a Tantrik tradition known for its use of human skulls in esoteric rites. In this panel, one can observe emaciated, almost skeletal figures engaged in arcane practices. At the top of the frame, three skulls are distinctly visible, as identified by temple guides. The central figure appears to hold a skull aloft, possibly using it as a bowl—an act symbolic of transcending mortal identity in Kapalika philosophy.

Such imagery offers valuable insight into the spiritual pluralism and ritual diversity of the time, revealing that Konark was not merely a temple of sun worship but also a vast canvas capturing the spiritual, social, and philosophical life of 13th-century India. Sadly, this intricate visual narrative is deteriorating rapidly. What was once a mountain of magnificent stone-carved storytelling is now at risk of fading into a heap of near-unidentifiable fragments. Without urgent attention, these rare portrayals—such as that of the Kapalikas—may be lost forever, taking with them untold chapters of India's sacred heritage.

The Turtle of Konark: Art in Utility

Among the many wonders of the Konark Sun Temple, what often goes unnoticed is its extraordinary integration of art and functionality, reflecting not only architectural brilliance but also a deep reverence for nature and biodiversity. A remarkable example lies in its water drainage system—a utilitarian feature transformed into a piece of living sculpture. In the image referenced, one can

observe a water outlet crafted in the form of a 'Makara', a mythological aquatic creature that symbolizes both fertility and cosmic energy in Indian tradition. Just beneath this Makara's gaping mouth, where the drained water would flow, is a beautifully sculpted turtle, positioned with such precision that it appears to be swimming through the outflow, creating a striking three-dimensional illusion of movement and life.

This clever interplay between engineering and artistic excellence reflects how the artisans of Konark infused even the most functional elements with aesthetic depth and symbolic meaning. The turtle, often associated with stability, longevity, and cosmic order, is not merely decorative—it is philosophically and ecologically resonant. Konark, thus, is not just a gallery of erotic sculptures as it is often popularly perceived. It is a living text in stone, where symbolism, sustainability, and artistic ingenuity converge. The temple offers a kaleidoscopic view of ancient Indian life, capturing everything from celestial alignments and ritual practices to flora, fauna, and mythological hybrids—all woven seamlessly into its architectural fabric.

Indeed, Konark is a monument to be experienced beyond the obvious, inviting explorers, scholars, and art lovers to look closely—where even a humble drain tells a story.

The Statues of Surya:

Central to the temple's spiritual and aesthetic narrative are the four statues of Surya, each embodying a distinct phase of the sun's daily journey. These sculptures are masterpieces of iconography, rich in symbolic and cultural significance. The statues of Surya are meticulously carved from chlorite stone, chosen for its durability and ability to capture intricate detail. Each of the four statues represents Surya at a different time of day: morning, midday, afternoon, and evening. The iconographic elements of these statues highlight Surya's role as the life-sustaining force of the universe.

Morning Sun: The statue of the morning Surya exudes a sense of calm and renewal. Surya is depicted standing upright, holding lotus flowers in his hands, symbolizing purity and the blossoming of life. The serene expression on his face reflects the gentle dawn light that awakens the world. This representation aligns with early Vedic traditions, where the morning sun is praised in hymns for its life-giving energy (Rigveda, 1.50.10).

Midday Sun: The midday Surya is the most prominent and richly adorned of the four statues. It portrays Surya in his full glory, radiating strength and vitality. The statue is accompanied by celestial attendants (dwarapalas), garland-bearing maidens, and prancing horses, symbolizing Surya's chariot journeying across the sky. The vigour of this depiction echoes the midday sun's role as the sustainer of life and agricultural productivity; themes celebrated in later Puranic texts such as the Surya Purana.

Afternoon Sun: This statue depicts a more subdued Surya, with a softened demeanour that reflects the sun's descent. The accompanying imagery, including attendants and horses, conveys a sense of transition and balance, emphasizing the cyclical nature of time and the sun's unceasing journey.

Evening Sun: The evening Surya is characterized by a tranquil and meditative expression. This statue symbolizes the fading light and the completion of the day's cycle. The artistic treatment of this phase underscore's themes of rest and rejuvenation, akin to the sun's nightly retreat into the cosmic ocean, a concept found in Vedic cosmology.

The four statues of Surya are deeply rooted in the Indian tradition of solar worship. In Vedic and post-Vedic literature, Surya is revered as the "eye of the universe" (Chandogya Upanishad, 3.19) and the source of all life. The alignment of the statues with the sun's movement underscores the temple's role as a cosmic observatory, integrating art, spirituality, and astronomy. The cyclical representation of Surya also reflects the ancient Indian concept of kala (time) as a continuous, ever-revolving phenomenon. The Konark Sun Temple was a significant centre for solar rituals. Devotees would circumambulate the temple, aligning their spiritual journey with the sun's path across the sky. The four statues served as focal points for worship at different times of the day, fostering a connection between human rhythms and cosmic cycles. The detailed carvings of the Surya statues exemplify the high point of Kalinga architecture. The regional style is evident in the intricate ornamentation, the dynamic poses of the celestial horses, and the harmonious integration of iconography with the temple's overall design. These statues highlight the syncretic blend of Vedic, Puranic, and local traditions in Odisha's art and architecture.

Vidalas of Konark: Guardians in Hybrid Forms

Among the many symbolic sculptural motifs that adorn the grandeur of ancient Indian temples, the *Vidala* (also known as *Vyala* or *Yali*) stands out as a formidable mythical creature. These composite beings—part animal, part human, often blending features of lions, elephants, horses, and even men—were traditionally believed to embody immense power, surpassing that of lions, tigers, or elephants. They served as protectors of sacred spaces, symbolizing the triumph of divine strength over chaos and evil. The Vidala motif manifests in various forms across India's temple architecture, but the Konark Sun Temple offers particularly striking and diverse examples. Carved in bold relief on its outer walls, these figures are not mere embellishments but carry deep metaphorical significance as guardians and enforcers of cosmic order.

In the attached image, we observe three distinct types of *Vidalas* represented in stone:

Simha Vidala *(left)* – A lion-headed creature, it is depicted ferociously subduing an elephant, signifying dominance over brute strength and unruly force.

Gaja Vidala *(center)* – This elephant-headed hybrid is shown trampling a human figure, emphasizing invincible might and authority.

Nara Vidala *(right)* – The rarest and intriguing of the trio, this human-headed Vidala is portrayed overpowering a fully armed warrior, perhaps symbolizing the victory of divine or higher intellect over worldly aggression.

Each of these figures exemplifies not only the sculptor's technical prowess but also the layered symbology embedded within temple art. Their dynamic postures and violent encounters evoke themes of vigilance, protection, and cosmic justice, acting as both literal and metaphorical gatekeepers of sacred space. The presence of such diverse Vidalas in Konark reflects the visionary artistry of the Eastern Ganga dynasty and the temple's place as a confluence of mythology, philosophy, and visual storytelling.

Image Caption:
Three distinct forms of Vidala sculptures on the outer walls of the Konark Sun Temple—(L) Simha Vidala overpowering an elephant, (C) Gaja Vidala crushing a human, and (R) the rare Nara Vidala trampling a warrior—each symbolizing divine dominance over worldly threats.

Female Composite Animals in Konark Art

One of the striking motifs in ancient Indian temple architecture is that of *composite animals*—mythical hybrids that blend the features of multiple creatures. Among the most recurring of these are the *Vidala* or *Vyala* figures, typically depicted as fierce, lion-like beings with ornamental flourish, often male in form. However, a closer examination of the sculptural program at the Konark Sun Temple reveals fascinating deviations from this norm. In the image attached, situated along the richly carved walls of this 13th-century marvel, we encounter a rare and exquisite pair of female composite beings. These figures, with their human upper torsos and leonine or animalistic lower bodies, may be aptly termed *Nari Vidalas*. They stand as a testimony to the nuanced imagination of the sculptors and their willingness to explore the feminine in even the most dynamic and symbolic motifs.

Such representations are not mere decorative anomalies; they suggest a layered aesthetic and symbolic worldview where feminine energy permeates even the realms of power, protection, and mysticism traditionally reserved for masculine imagery. These *Nari Vidalas* embody strength, beauty, and mythic hybridity—qualities often attributed to divine or supernatural forces in Indian iconography.

The presence of these rare figures underscores the importance of engaging with heritage sites like Konark not just through broad overviews but through intimate, detail-oriented observation. It is in these hidden corners and subtle carvings that the temple reveals its lesser-known stories—rich in imagination, cultural complexity, and artistic mastery—waiting to be rediscovered by the discerning eye.

Etched in Stone, Empowered in Spirit

The majestic walls of the Konark Sun Temple do more than narrate tales of celestial beauty and divine grandeur—they echo the timeless power, resilience, and agency of women in ancient Indian society. Among its myriads of intricate stone carvings is a striking portrayal of women engaged in *Mallayuddha*—traditional wrestling—a scene that challenges many modern assumptions about gender roles in antiquity. Far from being passive spectators in history, these women are shown as fierce competitors, physically agile and mentally resolute, asserting their presence in domains often deemed exclusive to men.

This powerful imagery, sculpted in the 13th century under the patronage of the Eastern Ganga dynasty, stands in sharp contrast to the restrictive norms that prevailed in other parts of the world for centuries—particularly in the realm of sports. While women's participation in global athletic events like the Olympics remained constrained well into the 20th century, here in ancient India, their strength was not only acknowledged but celebrated through temple art.

The Konark carvings are more than ornamental—they are social commentaries in stone, reflecting a world where women stood shoulder to shoulder with men, not as exceptions, but as equals. These depictions challenge us to reimagine history through a more inclusive lens, and to recognize that the empowerment of women is not a modern phenomenon—it is a legacy deeply rooted in our cultural past.

Śālabhañjikās of Konark: Grace Eternal in Stone

The Konark Sun Temple, a 13th-century marvel of Odisha, is not only a grand ode to Surya—the sun god—but also a breathtaking celebration of divine femininity. Among its most mesmerizing features are the *Śālabhañjikās*, or *Surasundarīs*—graceful female figures that ornament the temple's walls, pillars, and entrances. These celestial maidens, carved with exquisite delicacy, are far more than decorative elements—they embody the temple's artistic, spiritual, and symbolic essence.

Location and Placement: Where Beauty Meets Structure

The *Śālabhañjikās* are found throughout the Konark temple's architectural landscape:

- **On the janghas (walls)**: Integrated into friezes and

niches, often positioned rhythmically along the exterior.
- **Pillars and columns**: Carved in high relief, lending elegance and dynamism to the stone shafts.
- **Doorjambs and kapilis**: Adorning the junctions between the sanctum (*garbhagriha*) and the assembly hall (*jagamohana*), they signal a transition between earthly and divine space.

Types and Variations: A Gallery of Feminine Archetypes
While *Śālabhañjikā* literally means «a woman breaking a branch of a sal tree,» the broader category includes a pantheon of *Surasundarīs*, each embodying a distinct emotion or posture (*bhava* and *mudra*):
- **Alasā Kanya** (*Indolent Maiden*): Reclining in languor, suggesting dreamy introspection.

- **Torana Sundarī** (*Arch Maiden*): Standing gracefully beneath or holding an ornamental arch.
- **Māninī** (*Resentful Maiden*): With crossed arms and an averted gaze, expressing coy displeasure.

- **Guṇṭhanā** (*Bashful Maiden*): Eyes lowered, draped modestly, the very image of shyness.
- **Mugdhā** (*Innocent Maiden*): With childlike curiosity or naïve expression.
- **Vinyāsā** (*Contemplative Maiden*): Poised in meditative stillness, reflecting spiritual depth.

Iconography and Posture

The archetypal *Śālabhañjikā* is shown with one hand gently touching or bending a sal tree branch, an age-old motif in Indian sculpture that associates the maiden with fertility, renewal, and the vitality of nature. Others are seen:
- Applying kohl or arranging their hair
- Playing musical instruments or dancing
- Conversing with companions or taming animals

Each figure is animated with astonishing realism—subtle expressions, fluid body contours, and intricate jewelry speak of both technical mastery and narrative nuance.

These carvings are not mere indulgences in sensuality; they are deeply symbolic:
- **Feminine Shakti**: They represent the auspicious energy (*shakti*) essential for temple sanctity.
- **Devotional Imagery**: Their grace is equated with spiritual elevation—*sundarī* as an ideal devotee.
- **Aesthetic Rasa**: They embody *śṛṅgāra rasa* (the mood of love and beauty), believed to elevate the devotee›s consciousness through visual delight.
- **Architectural Balance**: The presence of feminine forms balances the solar masculinity of Surya with the gentleness of nature and the arts.

The *Śālabhañjikās* of Konark are enduring reminders of how ancient Indian art wove beauty, devotion, and symbolism into its sacred spaces. They celebrate the eternal feminine not as subordinate, but as integral to spiritual and cosmic balance. Carved from stone yet alive with rhythm and rasa, they continue to enchant and inspire.

Most of the stone sculptures at Konark now bear the marks of time—worn, weathered, and often fragmented. Yet, amid the ruins, a precious few still radiate the remarkable artistic brilliance of Odishan sculptors, standing as timeless testaments to their mastery.

"The Waiting Lady" or "The Lonely Lady," is one of Konark Sun Temple's most evocative creations. It portrays a woman leaning gracefully against a doorway, her serene face seemingly imbued with quiet hope—as though awaiting her beloved, perhaps a sculptor once toiling on the very temple that now houses her image. Despite centuries of weathering and decay, her expression endures—tender, timeless, and touched with an optimism that defies time.

King Narasimhadeva I: The Visionary Monarch of Konark

The sculpture portrays King Narasimhadeva I, the illustrious ruler of the Eastern Ganga dynasty, who reigned in the mid-13th century and envisioned the majestic Sun Temple at Konark. Renowned for his valour, devotion, and far-sighted leadership, Narasimhadeva combined the qualities of a warrior, statesman, and patron of art and architecture. In this remarkable panel, the King is depicted riding an elephant in a royal procession, armed with a bow, arrow, and shield—a vivid symbol of sovereignty, courage, and command. His entourage is seen presenting him with a giraffe, an extraordinary and exotic gift, beautifully carved in stone.

Beyond its aesthetic excellence, this sculpture serves as a historical narrative of a powerful and prosperous empire under Narasimhadeva's rule—an empire that upheld the ideals of strength, faith, and cultural sophistication, while maintaining dynamic global connections.

The rare statues of the Konark Sun Temple are not merely sculptural adornments but are living chronicles of Odisha's creative zenith in the 13th century. As we trace their intricate detailing, symbolic significance, and artistic finesse, we are drawn into a world where every chisel stroke carried meaning — spiritual, cosmic, or social. These statues, often overlooked amidst the temple's grand chariot form and colossal wheels, speak volumes about the aesthetic depth and philosophical sophistication of the Eastern Ganga dynasty.

From the majestic figure of Surya — the Sun God — radiating celestial energy, to the sensuous dancers, musicians, mythical beasts, and erotic couples, each rare sculpture at

Konark reveals a facet of life as understood in medieval Odisha. The sculptors not only celebrated the divine and the erotic but also subtly documented societal life, fashion, music, and the harmony between man and nature. Some of the rarest depictions — like the images of grieving women, forest dwellers, or unusual deities — widen the interpretive lens of scholars and art lovers alike.

In the erosion of many of these forms due to time and nature, what survives is not just stone but spirit — a persistent whisper of a civilization that dared to imagine beauty in bold and multifaceted ways. These rare statues are more than art; they are guardians of legacy, offering clues to ancient metaphysics, aesthetics, and cultural pluralism.

As we move forward to further chapters, let us carry with us the silent wisdom these statues impart — that art, when born of devotion and imagination, transcends time. Konark remains not just a monument, but a layered manuscript in stone — and its rare statues are some of its most precious verses.

References

- Behera, K. S. *Konark: The Heritage of Mankind.* Bhubaneswar: Aryan Books International, 1996.
- Donaldson, Thomas E. *Hindu Temple Art of Orissa, Vol. II: Konark.* Leiden: E.J. Brill, 1986.
- Panigrahi, Krishna Chandra. *Archaeological Remains at Bhubaneswar and Konark.* New Delhi: Archaeological Survey of India, 1961.
- Mishra, Krushna Chandra. *Konark: The Black Pagoda.* Cuttack: Vidyapuri, 1983.
- Nayak, Bishnu Charan. *Art and Iconography of the Sun*

- *Temple, Konark.* Bhubaneswar: Odisha State Museum, 2008.
- Donaldson, Thomas E. *The Iconography of the Buddhist Sculpture of Orissa.* New Delhi: Abhinav Publications, 2001.
- Mohapatra, R.P. *Archaeology in Orissa, Vol. I & II.* Delhi: B.R. Publishing Corporation, 1986.
- Sahu, N. K. *Konark: A Study of the Sun Temple of Orissa.* Bhubaneswar: Utkal University Press, 1956.
- Ray, Pratibha. *The Citadel of Love (Novel).* New Delhi: Rupa Publications, 2019.
- Kramrisch, Stella. *The Hindu Temple, Vol. II.* Delhi: Motilal Banarsidass, 1976.
- Information from Social Media.

Conservation Strategies for the Sun Temple

A colossal stone chariot frozen mid-gallop on the golden sands of Odisha, its twenty-four wheels still spinning in the imagination of every visitor who has ever stood before it. This is Konark—not just a temple, but a universe carved in stone, a cosmic question mark that has been haunting humanity for eight centuries.

The commissioning of the Sun Temple at Konark by King Narasimha Deva I in the 13th century was far more than a religious undertaking; it was a deliberate act of cultural and political expression. Conceived as a monumental chariot drawn by celestial horses, the temple was designed to embody the divine presence of Surya, the Sun God, within the earthly realm. This architectural vision not only reflects devotional intent but also articulates a sophisticated synthesis of cosmological symbolism, royal authority, and artistic excellence. In materializing the solar deity in such a monumental form, the temple becomes a powerful medium through which the king asserted both spiritual devotion and temporal sovereignty. Today, despite the ravages of time, the Konark Sun Temple continues to astonish. Its presence evokes not only the grandeur of medieval Odisha but also a deeper metaphysical ambition: to eternalize motion, divinity, and light through stone. Konark resists relegation to the status of a static monument. It remains culturally and symbolically alive, manifest in the annual dance festivals held in its precincts, in the ongoing scholarly attempts to interpret its iconography, and in conservation efforts aimed at preserving both its material structure and intangible heritage.

Early Conservation Initiatives for the preservation of the Konark Sun Temple dates back to 1803, when the East India Marine Board appealed to the Governor General of Bengal to initiate conservation measures. However, the response was minimal, resulting only in the prohibition of further stone removal from the site. This action, while symbolically significant, failed to halt the ongoing degradation of the structure.

In 1838, the Asiatic Society of Bengal reiterated concerns over the temple's deterioration. Nonetheless, tangible conservation actions remained limited to measures intended to deter vandalism, reflecting a reactive rather than proactive approach to heritage management. Between 1859 and 1894, various proposals to relocate or restore elements of the temple were floated. These attempts, however, were either abandoned due to logistical and financial constraints or halted in response to local opposition, signaling an early recognition of the cultural sensitivities associated with the site.

A turning point occurred in 1903, when the British administration undertook a major structural stabilization effort. The Jagamohana (assembly hall), already at risk of collapse, was filled with sand and sealed—a preventive measure designed to ensure the survival of the structure. This intervention, though not a restoration, marked the beginning of a more technically informed conservation strategy. In subsequent years, supplementary actions were carried out to repair the Mukhasala and Nata Mandir in 1905, and in 1906; Casuarina and tamanu trees were planted to mitigate damage from sand-laden coastal winds.

The post-independence period witnessed the institutionalization of conservation efforts under the aegis of the Archaeological Survey of India (ASI). Beginning in 1939, the ASI undertook systematic, long-term conservation initiatives, transitioning from the earlier colonial model of sporadic stabilization to a continuous process informed by emerging scientific techniques and international standards.

The legislative backbone of this transformation was the enactment of the *Ancient Monuments and Archaeological Sites and Remains Act* (AMASR Act) in 1958. This Act empowered the ASI with legal authority over the protection and management of heritage structures, including the Konark temple. The temple's inscription as a UNESCO World Heritage Site in 1984 further elevated its conservation status, bringing it under the purview of global heritage management frameworks.

Since the latter half of the 20th century, ASI has employed a range of scientific methodologies in its conservation programs at Konark. These include chemical surface cleaning, the use of paper pulp for delicate surface restoration, and stone consolidation techniques aimed at enhancing structural integrity. The ASI also implemented water drainage systems and periodic biocidal treatments to mitigate the effects of waterlogging and vegetative intrusion, respectively.

A significant component of ASI's contemporary strategy is the formulation and execution of Annual Conservation Plans, which enable ongoing monitoring and adaptive management of conservation activities. Under these plans, damaged structural elements are assessed, and targeted interventions are designed to ensure the temple's stability while maintaining material authenticity.

In accordance with ASI's 2014 conservation policy, new stone replacements follow a *"replacement policy"* wherein only plain stones are used to fill gaps left by deteriorated or missing ornamental blocks. This policy aims to differentiate modern additions from original material, preventing false historicism while reinforcing the structure.

One of the most ambitious recent undertakings is the Sand Removal Project, initiated in 2022, aimed at extracting the century-old sand infill from Jagamohana. Initially placed in 1903 to prevent collapse, the sand had begun to shift over time, creating voids that posed structural risks. Supported by structural studies from the Central Building Research Institute (CBRI), Roorkee, this project marks a paradigm shift—from passive stabilization to active restoration—underscoring the increasing reliance on scientific analysis in heritage management.

A central dilemma in the conservation of the Konark temple lies in balancing authenticity with structural stability. While the use of plain stone replacements provides a clear distinction between original and new materials, critics argue that this compromises the temple's aesthetic and historical coherence. Scholars and heritage professionals have called for a reconsideration of the ASI's policy, suggesting the incorporation of ornamental elements in restored sections to better reflect the temple's original grandeur. This debate reflects broader tensions in the field of conservation, where international charters such as the Venice Charter advocate for minimal intervention, while others emphasize the importance of visual and contextual fidelity in reconstruction.

Despite these advancements, the Konark Sun Temple remains vulnerable to a range of environmental and anthropogenic threats. Saline action from the nearby coast, heavy rainfall leading to waterlogging, biological colonization, and the encroachment of urban infrastructure continue to pose significant risks. Additionally, increasing tourism pressures necessitate the development of sustainable visitor management systems.

To address these challenges, the ASI has adopted five integrated management plans covering safety, environmental protection, master planning, environmental development, and tourism management—designed to preserve the temple's *Outstanding Universal Value* (OUV). These plans are periodically updated in alignment with recommendations from UNESCO and international heritage experts. Furthermore, international collaboration continues to play a vital role in shaping the conservation discourse. Expertise from global heritage institutions has informed of recent strategies aimed at mitigating the long-term effects of climate change, pollution, and human activity.

What began as reactive, ad hoc efforts during the colonial period has transformed into a comprehensive, scientifically informed, and internationally coordinated conservation regime. As new technologies and preservation philosophies emerge, the ongoing challenge remains to protect the temple's structural integrity while honoring its historical authenticity. Continued dialogue among conservators, scholars, policymakers, and the public will be essential to ensure that the legacy of Konark endures for future generations.

In 1984, the Konark Sun Temple received international recognition through its inclusion in the UNESCO World Heritage List. The designation cited the temple as "a masterpiece of creative genius" and "a unique artistic achievement," accurately capturing the monument's architectural and cultural significance. This recognition marked a pivotal moment in Konark's modern history, affirming its transition from a national treasure to a site of global heritage. With this new status came both opportunities and obligations: enhanced visibility, increased funding, international collaboration, and a framework of responsibilities rooted in UNESCO's principles of safeguarding "Outstanding Universal Value."

This milestone of international recognition transformed the conservation landscape at Konark. The temple was no longer merely India's cultural asset; it became a shared inheritance of humanity. As such, India assumed new responsibilities, including the enforcement of protective legislation, regular condition monitoring, the facilitation of sustainable tourism, and the maintenance of Outstanding Universal Value in line with UNESCO's standards. These requirements initiated a paradigm shift from reactive preservation to proactive, science-led conservation.

Following the UNESCO designation, the conservation of Konark entered a new phase characterized by interdisciplinary collaboration. Institutions such as the Indian National Trust for Art and Cultural Heritage

(INTACH), IIT Bhubaneswar, Harvard University's Center for Conservation Studies, and numerous European and North American research bodies began contributing expertise. This marked a shift from conservation as a national duty to a model of global stewardship, wherein Konark served as both a case study and a laboratory for testing innovative preservation techniques.

Today's conservation efforts at Konark employ tools and methodologies that would appear magical to the 13th-century artisans who constructed the temple. 3D laser scanning facilitates the creation of digital twins for structural analysis, while photogrammetry produces high-resolution three-dimensional models from photographic data. Ground-penetrating radar (GPR) identifies sub-surface features, and environmental monitoring systems continuously track microclimatic factors such as temperature, humidity, and pollutant levels.

Material science and archaeometry support these efforts by analyzing stone fatigue and diagnosing micro-fractures and chemical deterioration. These tools provide unprecedented insights into the temple's vulnerabilities and allow conservationists to develop predictive models for long-term preservation.

Konark in the 21st Century

Today, the Konark Sun Temple functions not only as a cultural symbol but also as a global model for integrated heritage conservation. The fusion of traditional craftsmanship with modern conservation science has positioned Konark at the forefront of experimental heritage management. Through sustained collaboration among governmental agencies, academic institutions, and international partners, Konark exemplifies how monuments of antiquity can be preserved using future-facing methodologies—without sacrificing the authenticity and spirit that renders them timeless.

What is particularly noteworthy is the philosophical shift in the purpose of conservation itself. The goal is no longer to freeze monuments in time but to maintain their continuity. Technology here is not merely a tool of preservation; it becomes an instrument of reverence. The scientific gaze aligns with cultural devotion, allowing Konark to continue inspiring and transforming those who encounter it.

Today, Konark faces challenges that would make even the most optimistic conservator wake up in cold sweats. The temple that has survived eight centuries of monsoons, invasions, and neglect now faces threats that are both more subtle and more dangerous than anything in its past. Climate change isn't just an abstract environmental concern—it's an immediate threat to Konark's survival. Rising sea levels and increasingly erratic weather patterns create cycles of expansion and contraction that stress ancient masonry designed for more predictable conditions. The chlorite and laterite stones are corroding faster due to acidic rain and salt-laden winds, while temperature fluctuations create micro-fractures that compound over time.

Then there's the tourism paradox. Over a million visitors annually bring economic benefits but also noise, pollution, and physical wear. The infrastructure needed to accommodate these numbers sometimes conflicts with conservation priorities. How do you balance accessibility with preservation? How do you welcome the world without destroying what they've come to see?

Urban encroachment presents another challenge. Local commercialization and development are disrupting the visual and cultural context of the monument. Hotels, shops, and tourist facilities alter the site's atmosphere and create new sources of pollution and congestion. The temple that once stood in splendid isolation now finds itself surrounded by the detritus of modern tourism.

Invasive flora creates problems that earlier conservators never imagined. Roots from encroaching trees and plants destabilize stone foundations, create cracks that allow water penetration, and require constant, expert attention to manage. The vegetation that makes the site beautiful also threatens its structural integrity.

Perhaps most challenging are the philosophical questions that have no easy answers. Should missing parts be reconstructed or left as evocative ruins? How much tourist infrastructure is appropriate? Should the sand-filled Jagamohana be excavated using new technologies, or would that create unacceptable risks? Different conservation philosophies suggest different answers, and the stakes couldn't be higher.

This is where Konark's story becomes truly remarkable. The temple has evolved beyond its original function as a place of worship to become something unprecedented: a cultural ecosystem that nurtures multiple forms of artistic expression while maintaining its spiritual and historical significance.

The annual dance festival is just the most visible manifestation of this evolution. The temple also hosts sand art festivals on nearby Chandrabhaga Beach, where international artists create temporary sculptures that reference the temple's themes while addressing contemporary concerns. Educational programs bring thousands of schoolchildren to the site annually, creating new generations of cultural custodians. Heritage walks, digital apps, and online courses make the temple's history and significance accessible to global audiences.

This approach to heritage preservation—through active cultural engagement rather than protective isolation—represents a fundamental shift in conservation philosophy. The temple survives not just through physical maintenance but through its continued ability to inspire, educate, and transform those who encounter it. The economic impact extends far beyond tourism revenue. Local artisans who maintain traditional skills in stone carving, textile work, and other decorative arts find new markets and recognition through festival activities. The hospitality sector benefits from visitor influx while local cultural organizations participate in year-round programming and preparation activities.

But perhaps most importantly, this approach maintains the temple's cultural relevance. When contemporary dancers perform against the backdrop of stone sculptures, when artists create modern interpretations of ancient themes, when scholars from around the world collaborate on conservation research, Konark remains a living part of human culture rather than a museum piece preserved in artificial isolation.

This brings us to the heart of the matter: what exactly are we trying to preserve? Is it the stones themselves, arranged in their current configuration? Is it the artistic vision of the original builders? Is it the cultural meanings that have accumulated over centuries? Or is it something more ineffable—the temple's capacity to move, inspire, and transform those who encounter it?

Different conservation philosophies suggest different answers. The minimal intervention principle, influenced by international conservation charters, advocates preserving what exists without speculative rebuilding, recognizing that evidence of age and historical change is itself culturally valuable. Community-centered conservation emphasizes local involvement and recognizes that heritage sites exist within living cultural contexts. Cultural sustainability seeks to align conservation with artistic revival and contemporary cultural expression.

The most successful conservation efforts at Konark have been those that recognize the site as a living cultural resource rather than a static historical artifact. The integration of physical preservation with cultural programming, exemplified by the dance festival and related activities, represents a model for heritage management that other sites worldwide are beginning to emulate.

This philosophy acknowledges that effective conservation isn't about "fixing" heritage sites or returning them to some imagined original state. Instead, it's about maintaining their capacity to generate meaning, foster community, and inspire creative expression. It's about making ourselves worthy of the artistic vision and cultural legacy these monuments represent.

The ethical dimensions of this approach are complex. How do we balance authenticity with accessibility? How do we respect traditional values while embracing contemporary interpretations? How do we serve local communities while meeting international conservation standards?

These questions have no simple answers, but they must be continuously negotiated through dialogue between diverse stakeholders.

The digital transformation of heritage conservation has opened possibilities that would have seemed magical to earlier generations of conservators. High-quality virtual tours allow people who cannot visit physically to explore the site in detail. Augmented reality applications overlay historical information and reconstructions onto the actual site experience. Online archives make research and documentation accessible to global scholarly communities. But digital technology isn't just about creating alternatives to physical visits; it is about enhancing understanding and engagement for all audiences. Mobile applications provide interactive guides with historical information, architectural analysis, and augmented reality features.

The documentation capabilities of digital technology are particularly significant. 3D scanning and photogrammetry produce data that is more precise and comprehensive than traditional methods. This documentation serves multiple purposes: it creates permanent records that can track changes over time, it provides data for structural analysis and conservation planning, and it preserves detailed information that future generations can use in ways we cannot yet imagine.

Digital platforms also facilitate collaboration between researchers, conservators, and cultural practitioners worldwide. Shared databases and online research tools enable coordinated conservation efforts and scholarly exchange that would have been impossible in earlier eras. The temple has become a node in global networks of heritage conservation and cultural research.

The economic dimensions of heritage conservation at Konark reveal the complex relationships between cultural value and economic impact. The temple attracts over a million visitors annually, generating significant revenue for local communities and the regional economy. The dance festival alone creates economic opportunities that extend far beyond ticket sales—accommodation, transportation, food services, handicrafts, and cultural programming all benefit from the influx of cultural tourists.

But managing these economic benefits requires careful balancing. Tourism revenue can support conservation efforts, but tourism pressure can accelerate deterioration. Cultural programming can maintain the site's relevance, but inappropriate programming can compromise its integrity. Local economic development can provide incentives for heritage preservation, but uncontrolled development can destroy the cultural context that makes heritage sites meaningful.

The festival and related cultural activities support local cultural industries including handicrafts, textiles, music, and dance. These industries provide employment opportunities while maintaining traditional skills and knowledge that might otherwise disappear. The economic value of cultural continuity is difficult to quantify but impossible to overstate.

International recognition through UNESCO designation and cultural programming enhances India's soft power and cultural diplomacy efforts. The festival serves as a showcase for Indian cultural achievement that influences international perceptions and relationships. This diplomatic value translates into practical benefits through increased tourism, cultural exchange opportunities, and international cooperation on conservation projects. The communities surrounding Konark have their own relationships with the temple that often differ from those of tourists, scholars, or government officials. For residents, the temple is not just a tourist attraction or research subject—it's part of the landscape of daily life, a presence that shapes identity and provides economic opportunities.

Traditional craftspeople whose ancestors may have worked on the original construction maintain skills and knowledge that are invaluable for conservation efforts. Their understanding of traditional materials, techniques, and structural principles provides insights that cannot be obtained through purely scientific analysis. Recent conservation efforts have begun to recognize and incorporate this traditional knowledge, creating partnerships between modern conservation science and ancient craftsmanship.

The festival and related cultural activities create opportunities for local participation that go beyond economic benefits. Young people from the area participate in cultural programming, learning traditional arts and crafts that connect them with their heritage. Local cultural organizations contribute to festival programming and year-round activities that maintain cultural continuity.

But community involvement also raises questions about cultural ownership and control. Whose heritage is Konark? How should decisions about the future be made? How can local voices be heard in forums dominated by government officials, international experts, and cultural institutions? These questions are particularly relevant as heritage sites have become increasingly integrated into global tourism and cultural exchange networks.

The most successful aspects of Konark's conservation and cultural programming have been those that genuinely engage local communities as partners rather than passive beneficiaries. This engagement requires ongoing dialogue, mutual respect, and willingness to adapt programs based on community feedback and changing needs.

Looking toward the future, Konark faces both opportunities and challenges that will shape its continued evolution. Climate change will require adaptive conservation strategies that can respond to changing environmental conditions while maintaining the site's integrity. Emerging technologies including artificial intelligence and advanced materials science offer new possibilities for conservation and visitor engagement, but implementing these technologies requires careful consideration of their cultural appropriateness and long-term sustainability.

The growing recognition of cultural heritage as a driver of sustainable development creates new opportunities for funding and support, but also new pressures to demonstrate economic returns on heritage investment. The challenge will be maintaining the balance between economic utility and cultural authenticity that has made Konark's conservation efforts successful.

Global partnerships will become increasingly important as heritage sites face challenges that transcend national boundaries. Climate change, technological disruption, and cultural homogenization require collaborative responses that draw on diverse expertise and resources. Konark's experience with international collaboration provides a model for other sites facing similar challenges.

The next generation of heritage professionals will

need to be equally comfortable with traditional conservation methods and cutting-edge technology, equally versed in local cultural contexts and global conservation standards. They will need to be diplomats as well as technicians, able to navigate complex relationships between diverse stakeholders while maintaining focus on heritage preservation goals.

Perhaps most importantly, future heritage conservation will need to maintain the spirit of innovation and cultural engagement that has made Konark's recent evolution so successful. The temple that began as a cosmic chariot designed to capture the sun's eternal dance has become a modern laboratory for exploring the relationships between past and present, tradition and innovation, local identity and global heritage.

So here we are, eight centuries after King Narasimhadeva -I first dreamed of caging the sun in stone, still grappling with the same fundamental questions about art, time, and human aspiration. Konark remains what it has always been: a mirror that reflects our deepest hopes and fears about our capacity to create meaning in the face of impermanence. The temple's wheels no longer turn in their original cosmic dance, but they continue to move us. They move conservators to develop new technologies for preservation. They move dancers to create new interpretations of ancient themes. They move scholars to ask new questions about the relationships between architecture and culture. They move communities to maintain traditions while embracing change.

Perhaps this is the real secret of Konark's conservation: it survives not because we have successfully preserved it, but because it continues to preserve something essential about human creativity and aspiration. It reminds us that the urge to create, to build, to leave something beautiful for future generations is as fundamental to human nature as the urge to survive.

Conservation and preservation is not about making heritage sites eternal, nothing is eternal. It is about making them meaningful, ensuring they continue to inspire, challenge, and transform those who encounter them. If we can preserve Konark's capacity to generate wonder, to bring people together across cultural and temporal boundaries, and to provoke new forms of creative expression, then perhaps we have conserved something more valuable than stone.

The sun rises each day over Konark, just as it has been for eight centuries. The dance continues. The questions endure. And somewhere in the space between stone and spirit, past and future, the eternal conversation between human aspiration and cosmic mystery continues to unfold.

The chariot wheels may rest in stone, but the spirit of the journey dances on — come, witness eternal grace at the Konark Dance Festival."

References
- Archaeological Survey of India (ASI). *Annual Report 2014–2023*. New Delhi: Ministry of Culture, Government of India.
- Basu, R.N. (1994). *Conservation of Konarak: A Study in Cultural Management*. New Delhi: Agam Kala Prakashan.
- Bevan, Robert. (2006). *The Destruction of Memory: Architecture at War.* London: Reaktion Books.
- CBRI (Central Building Research Institute). (2018).

- *Structural Stability Report on Konark Sun Temple (2013–2018).* Roorkee: CSIR-CBRI.
- Fergusson, James. (1876). *History of Indian and Eastern Architecture.* London: John Murray.
- INTACH (Indian National Trust for Art and Cultural Heritage). (2020). *Heritage Management and Conservation at Konark.* Bhubaneswar: INTACH Odisha Chapter.
- Jigyasu, Rohit. (2002). *Reducing Disaster Vulnerability through Local Knowledge: The Case of Earthquake-Prone Rural Communities in India and Nepal.* Trondheim: NTNU.
- Kaul, Suraj B. (1997). "Modern Techniques in the Conservation of Historic Monuments in India." *Studies in Conservation,* Vol. 42(2): 85–90.
- Lahiri, Nayanjot. (2012). *Ashoka in Ancient India.* Cambridge, MA: Harvard University Press.
- Mishra, Ramesh Prasad. (2019). "Paper Pulp Cleaning Method for Sandstone Surfaces: Application at Konark Temple." *Journal of Conservation Science,* Vol. 35(3): 215–222.
- Smith, Laurajane. (2006). *Uses of Heritage.* London: Routledge.
- UNESCO World Heritage Centre. (1984). *World Heritage Nomination: Konark Sun Temple (India).* Paris: UNESCO.
- UNESCO. (2013). *Managing Cultural World Heritage: World Heritage Resource Manual.* Paris: UNESCO World Heritage Centre.

The Konark Dance Festival

"Art is eternal. Art connects us —across time, space, and culture."

Located on the east coast of India, in a town where the timeless rhythm of the sea meets the pulse of history, one visionary transformed the cultural landscape. For Guru Gangadhar Pradhan, dance was far more than a means of self-expression—it was an intimate communion with the divine. He dreamed of reimagining his native town, Konark, which was already renowned for its majestic Sun Temple, into one of the greatest hubs of culture and art. Konark's ancient Sun Temple, an awe-inspiring example of 13th-century Kalinga architecture and a designated UNESCO World Heritage Site, stands as a symbol of India's rich heritage and devotion to Surya, the Sun God. Yet Guru Pradhan saw beyond its architectural grandeur. He envisioned a way to bring the temple to life through the vibrant expressions of dance and music. This insight sparked the creation of the Konark Dance Festival in 1986—a bold initiative designed to popularize India's classical dance traditions and to place Konark firmly on the global cultural map.

History and Evolution of the Konark Dance Festival
The festival evolved into the Konark Music and Dance

Festival (Konark Natya Mandap), a collaborative effort involving the Odisha Government, the Odisha Tourism Development Corporation (OTDC), and the Department of Culture. The festival's primary objectives are twofold: to celebrate and propagate Odissi—the classical dance form of Odisha—and to showcase the magnificent Sun Temple. By drawing tourists to Konark, the festival not only boosts local cultural pride and economic development but also reinforces a deep sense of cultural self-esteem. Odissi, which was on the brink of extinction in the early twentieth century, has been revived through the persistent efforts of cultural custodians like Guru Pradhan. The Konark Dance Festival has served as a fortress for this ancient art form, ensuring its survival and flourishing on the contemporary stage. The festival has transcended the boundaries of a traditional cultural event. It has become a propagator of creative ground for artistic ventures. In these moments of mutual learning and creative exchange, the Konark Music and Dance Festival has evolved into a transformative platform. It not only celebrates the past but also catalyses future artistic innovation, forging a vibrant link between tradition and modernity.

In essence, Guru Gangadhar Pradhan's vision has redefined Konark as a beacon of cultural resurgence—where the eternal dance of art continues to unite humanity across the ages. As the festival progressed, its reputation grew exponentially, transforming itself from a regional celebration into a world-famous centre for global cultural exchange. This indigenous festivity, which showcases India's classical dances, has become an amalgamation of ideas, styles, and traditions. Artists not only display their masterpieces but also engage in a dynamic exchange of cultural insights with participants from diverse civilizations.

Once known as a serene temple town, Konark has evolved into an energetic hub of creativity and cultural dialogue. Set against the breath-taking backdrop of the ancient Sun Temple, the festival has become a major tourist hotspot and a revered pilgrimage site for art lovers and dance admirers alike. The temple's intricate sculptures and timeless grandeur infuse the event with a profound historical and spiritual connection, adding an extra layer of depth to the performances. In this vibrant setting, the performing arts serve as a powerful vehicle for transmitting India's rich cultural heritage. Through evocative renditions steeped in myth, spirituality, and folklore, artists bring ancient epics and religious traditions to life, ensuring that the legacy of classical dance and music continues to flourish on the global stage.

The sculptures at the Konark Sun Temple offer a fascinating glimpse into the ancient cultural landscape of dance and music. They not only preserve the memory of a rich artistic tradition but also underscore the importance of sustaining these art forms for future generations. The temple walls vividly illustrate various forms of dance, showcasing figures engaged in expressive and dynamic movements. One prominent type is the Nartaki (dancer). In these sculptures, the dancer is shown with one leg crossed behind the other, capturing the fluid motion of a dance that seems to transcend time. As described in texts like the *Shilpa Prakasha*, the dancer appears as a celestial damsel—lost in the rhythm of her performance, embodying both grace and divine beauty.

The depiction of dance in Konark is rooted in a long-standing tradition that dates back to the Indus Valley Civilization, where the earliest images of dancing women have been found. Over time, these simple figures evolved into more elaborate representations, with detailed portrayals of various dance postures. The intricate dispositions of the hands, legs, and feet in these sculptures—referred to as *sthanas* or *karanas*—each carry specific meanings. Sanskrit literature, notably Bharata's *Natyashastra*, meticulously describes these karanas, highlighting the technical and expressive aspects of dance. A verse from *Kalidasa's Malvikagnimitra* poetically encapsulates the beauty of a dancer, a sentiment that resonates with the sculptures' lifelike depiction of movement.

In addition to the general portrayal of dancers, the temple features distinct types of female figures known as *Alasa kanyas*. These figures are artistically rendered to exhibit various moods and styles of dance: As discussed in the *Shilpa Prakasha*, one type of Alasa kanya is portrayed with one leg crossed behind the other, embodying the dynamic movement of dance. Her graceful posture and serene expression evoke the image of a celestial maiden, immersed in her art. This figure is depicted holding a lotus bud in her right hand, with her knees slightly bent in a delicate pose that suggests she is either putting on or removing her anklet bells. In Sanskrit literature, such imagery is linked to the idea of a vassaksajjika Nayika—one who adorns herself with ornaments and attentively prepares for the arrival of her lover. The scene of adjusting anklets, described in classical texts, is beautifully mirrored in the temple's sculptures. Unique among the *alasa kanyas, the mardala* is the only musician in this group. Her head is gently tilted, and her features convey the deep concentration of a musician lost in her performance. In front of her, a drum is depicted, symbolizing the integral role of rhythm in the classical dance tradition.

The extensive exploration of dance by ancient Indian sculptors is evident in the detailed depiction of these figures on the temple walls. The various postures and gestures, whether in the form of delicate hand movements or the dynamic placement of feet, represent a codified language of dance that has been passed down through generations. Vatsyayan, a renowned scholar, observes that the dance sculptures in Odisha effectively capture the *caris* (dance steps) detailed in the *Natyashastra*. Dramaturg Nadikeshvara, in his treatise *Abhinayadarpana*, further elaborates on the ideal state of the female dancer, emphasizing qualities such as slenderness, beauty, and fluid movement—characteristics that are vividly brought to life in these sculptures.

The nuanced expressions and postures found in Konark's art form a visual lexicon that communicates the emotional depth and technical precision of ancient Indian dance. The temple's sculptural program, deeply rooted in the traditions of Odishan art, reflects both universal and local sensibilities. With a strong influence from Tantrism and the Shakta cults, the rich and often complex portrayal of female imagery—both secular and semi-divine—has become a defining characteristic of Odishan temple architecture. This regional style, while honouring long-standing traditions, also allowed for unique artistic expressions that set the temples of Orissa apart. In essence, the dance and music sculptures of the Konark Sun Temple do more than depict artistic forms; they serve as a testament to a cultural heritage that celebrates movement, emotion, and the eternal beauty of artistic expression. Through these intricate carvings, the past comes alive, inviting us to appreciate and continue the legacy of Growth and Expansion:

From Local to International – The Journey of the Konark Dance Festival

The Konark Dance Festival stands as a testament to India's rich cultural heritage, evolving from a local initiative to an internationally recognized platform for classical dance and music. Its journey, marked by growth, diversification, and resilience, reflects a deep commitment to preserving and promoting India's artistic traditions.

The Inception : 1986

The Konark Dance Festival was founded by Guru Gangadhar Pradhan, a visionary Odissi exponent, with the aim of promoting India's classical dance forms and establishing Konark as a global cultural landmark. His vision was to create a prestigious platform that would celebrate and showcase the rich artistic traditions of India. The festival was set against the majestic backdrop of the Sun Temple of Konark. The temple's historical grandeur and spiritual aura added a sense of divinity and artistic depth to the performances, making the festival an immersive cultural experience. While the festival primarily highlighted Odissi, the classical dance form of Odisha, it also featured performances of other Indian classical dance traditions, including Bharatanatyam, Kathak, Manipuri, and Mohiniattam. This diversity not only celebrated India's multifaceted cultural heritage but also made the festival a melting pot of artistic expression, attracting dancers and enthusiasts from across the country. The Konark Dance Festival was thus conceived as a grand confluence of tradition, history, and artistic excellence, laying the foundation for its future growth as one of India's most prestigious cultural events.

Early Development and Institutional Recognition :1987-1990

The Konark Dance Festival experienced significant growth and recognition at the national level, drawing attention from artists, scholars, and cultural enthusiasts across India. The festival's unique setting, with the Sun Temple of Konark as its breathtaking backdrop, played a crucial role in its rising popularity. The temple's intricate sculptures and architectural grandeur seemed to come alive under the glow of the evening lights, creating an enchanting atmosphere that captivated both performers and audiences alike. As the festival gained prominence, it expanded beyond traditional performances to include workshops, seminars, and interactive cultural sessions. These additions transformed the event from a mere dance showcase into a holistic cultural experience, fostering a deeper engagement with India's classical arts. The festival became a platform for knowledge exchange, where renowned dancers, musicians, and scholars shared their insights, enriching the artistic community and inspiring the next generation of performers.

The Konark Dance Festival laid the groundwork for its evolution into a premier cultural event, setting the stage for its expansion beyond national boundaries in the coming years with its growing reputation and increasing participation.

Expanding Influence :1991-1995

During this period, the Konark Dance Festival expanded its reach, transitioning from a nationally recognized event to an internationally acclaimed cultural festival.

The festival's growing prestige attracted international artists and performers, marking its emergence onto the global stage. Dancers and musicians from various countries began participating, introducing cross-cultural artistic exchanges that enriched the festival's creative landscape. This global recognition elevated Konark's status as a major hub for classical performing arts. The festival expanded to include a broader range of Indian classical dance traditions, such as Bharatanatyam, Kathak, Manipuri, Mohiniattam, Kuchipudi, Kathakali, and Sattriya in addition to Odissi. This diversity not only showcased India's vast cultural heritage but also provided audiences with a comprehensive experience of the country's dance traditions. The festival introduced traditional Indian classical music to enhance the artistic experience , featuring instrumental and vocal performances alongside dance presentations to enhance the artistic experience and accompaniment using instruments such as the sitar, flute, veena, tabla, mridangam, and pakhawaj added depth and resonance, making the performances more immersive and emotionally engaging. The festival became a platform for cross-cultural dialogue, fostering creative collaborations between Indian and global artists with the participation of international performers. These interactions led to a fusion of artistic influences, broadening the festival's creative scope while maintaining the authenticity and essence of Indian classical arts. The Konark Dance Festival had firmly established itself as a global cultural event, attracting renowned artists, scholars, and audiences from around the world. Its commitment to preserving traditional Indian arts while embracing global influences ensured its continued growth and influence on the international stage. The Konark Dance Festival had firmly established itself as a prestigious international event, attracting global audiences, scholars, and performers while continuing to celebrate and preserve India's artistic heritage by the mid 1990.

The Konark Dance Festival organically expanded to include classical music recitals, especially Hindustani and Carnatic, leading to its informal naming as the **Konark Music and Dance Festival.** This phase reflected a rich cultural integration of Indian performing arts, blending *sangeet* (music) and *nritya* (dance) into a unified artistic experience.

A Decade of Excellence :1996

The Konark Music and Dance Festival. celebrated its tenth anniversary in 1996, marking a decade of artistic brilliance and cultural significance. The festival had firmly established itself as one of India's leading platforms for classical dance and music. Its grand setting, combined with the artistic excellence of participating performers, made it a hallmark event in the country's cultural calendar by tenth edition. .This festival's reputation is extended beyond national borders with attraction of international attention and participation. The number of participating artists grew significantly, reflecting the festival's rising prominence in the performing arts community. Renowned dancers from across India and beyond took part in the event, further enhancing its artistic credibility. Alongside this, the spectator count saw a dramatic rise, drawing larger audiences comprising dance enthusiasts, tourists, and cultural scholars. This influx solidified Konark's position as a major cultural destination, with the festival serving as a key attraction for visitors from around the world. The festival not only enriched India's artistic landscape but also contributed to Konark's recognition as a global heritage and cultural hub. The growing audience base and increased participation played a crucial role in promoting Odisha's rich traditions, dance heritage, and architectural splendour, further boosting tourism in the region. The Konark Music and Dance Festival stood as a shining beacon of India's classical arts, paving the way for even greater international recognition and artistic collaborations in the years to come with a decade of remarkable achievements.

Achieving Global Recognition :1997-2005

By the 1990s, the Konark Dance Festival had gained considerable national and international attention, gradually evolving into a prestigious cultural platform that celebrated the richness of Indian classical arts. This period marked a turning point, as the festival began to attract renowned dancers, musicians, scholars, and connoisseurs from around the world, transforming the event into a vibrant melting pot of artistic expression.

With increasing international participation, the festival became a site of cross-cultural collaboration, where artists from diverse backgrounds shared the stage with Indian classical performers. These interactions fostered a deeper global appreciation for India's rich performing arts heritage, while also encouraging cultural diplomacy and artistic innovation.

To enhance the festival's artistic depth, classical music performances—including Hindustani and Carnatic vocal and instrumental recitals—were introduced alongside the dance presentations. This not only added a rich auditory layer to the visual spectacle but also emphasized the intrinsic connection between Indian classical music (sangeet) and dance (nritya).

Recognizing the need for knowledge exchange and artistic development, the festival also incorporated workshops, lecture-demonstrations, and interactive sessions. These programs allowed emerging dancers, musicians, and researchers to engage with established gurus and scholars, turning the festival into a vibrant learning environment and a space for cultural dialogue and mentorship.

By the early 2000s, the festival had firmly established itself as a global hub for Indian classical performing arts, bridging the realms of tradition and modernity, national and international audiences, and performers and learners alike.

Since the 2000s, the event has been expanding its

scope beyond classical dance and music. Organized by the Odisha Tourism Department in collaboration with the Odisha Sangeet Natak Akademi, the festival now includes crafts fairs, handloom exhibitions, food festivals, and the International Sand Art Festival held at Chandrabhaga Beach. This evolution has enriched the festival's cultural appeal and strengthened its position as a major tourism and cultural event on the global calendar.

The 20th Anniversary – A Global Beacon of Indian Classical Arts : 2006

The Konark Dance Festival had firmly established itself as a prestigious global platform for Indian classical dance and music by its 20th anniversary. The festival had become an annual pilgrimage for artists and connoisseurs of classical dance and music by setting against the majestic backdrop of the sun temple and reinforcing its stature in the global arts community. The 20th edition featured special performances by legendary artists, paying tribute to the rich legacy of Indian classical dance and music to commemorate this momentous occasion. These performances not only honoured tradition but also showcased the festival's evolution, blending time-honoured dance forms with contemporary interpretations within the classical framework.

A key highlight of the festival was the homage paid to its visionary founder, **Guru Gangadhar Pradhan**, whose relentless dedication and artistic vision had transformed Konark into a global cultural hub. Tributes and commemorative events were organized in his honour, with artists, students, and scholars expressing their gratitude for his pioneering contributions. His efforts had shaped the festival into a globally respected institution, leaving a lasting impact on the world of Indian classical arts. The Konark Dance Festival was no longer just a national event; it had grown into a celebrated international platform, fostering cultural exchange, artistic excellence, and a deep appreciation for India's classical traditions. Its success reaffirmed Konark's place on the world cultural map, ensuring its continued growth and influence in the years to come by 2006.

Evolution into the Konark and Dance Festival :2007-2017

The Konark Dance Festival, held annually against the backdrop of the iconic Sun Temple in Konark, Odisha, has undergone notable evolution between 2007 and 2017.The festival originated in 1989 and, by the 2000s, had become a mainstay event from December 1–5 each year, emphasizing Indian classical dances and Odisha's tourism appeal.

Throughout 2007-2017, the festival retained its five-day format, featuring leading exponents of dance forms such as Odissi, Bharatanatyam, Kathak, Kuchipudi, Manipuri, Mohiniattam, and Sattriya. Early years focused on solo and duet performances, but, by this decade, the scale and diversity of participation increased, regularly featuring international troupes and collaborative productions. The event not only showcased classical dances but also celebrated folk and tribal performances, enhancing cultural integration and visibility for Odisha's heritage.

Eminent artists from across the nation and, increasingly, abroad—especially from Southeast Asia—brought greater internationalization to the festival.

Since the mid-2010s, particularly from 2015

onwards, the International Sand Art Festival was organized concurrently with the dance festival on Chandrabhaga Beach, welcoming artists from across India and multiple other countries. Parallel events included the Crafts Mela or Artist Camp, promoting Orissan temple sculpture, handlooms, and crafts; these exhibitions and markets ran alongside the main dance performances and highlighted regional artisanship.

The festival played a key role in reviving Odisha's unique dance traditions by integrating them into mainstream cultural consciousness and nurturing the Odissi dance's national and international status. Over 2007–2017, the festival evolved into a vibrant platform for cultural diplomacy, inter-state collaborations, and as a significant tourist draw for Odisha.

The open-air auditorium, continuing as the iconic venue in front of the historic temple, enhanced the connection between dance art and architectural heritage, furthering the narrative of Odisha as a living treasury of art and tradition.

The festival remained continuous and largely unchanged in structure, but its content and collaborative spirit broadened, fostering both the regional and pan-Indian aspects of classical dance heritage. By 2017, the Konark Dance Festival had solidified its place not only as a preserver of tradition but as a globally-recognized venue for choreographed heritage and cultural exchange. Overall, the Konark Dance Festival from 2007 to 2017 emphasizes Odisha's ongoing commitment to sustaining, broadening, and contextualizing Indian dance traditions—turning the event into both a monument-focused celebration and an evolving cultural bridge.

Growth and Diversification : 2017–2020

The Konark Festival moved into its fourth decade, it continued to evolve and expand, embracing contemporary artistic influences while remaining deeply rooted in India's classical traditions. This period was marked by increased engagement with younger audiences, greater experimentation with artistic forms, and enhanced global collaborations, making the festival more dynamic and inclusive than ever before. The festival introduced new elements within the classical framework to engage younger generations, ensuring that the essence of Indian dance and music remained intact while being accessible to modern audiences. Digital innovations, interactive sessions, and educational outreach programs encouraged aspiring dancers and musicians to explore the depth and beauty of classical arts. One of the most significant developments during this phase was the growing number of cross-cultural collaborations. Indian classical dancers and musicians partnered with international artists, resulting in innovative fusion performances that combined traditional Indian styles with global influences such as ballet, jazz, flamenco, and contemporary dance. These collaborations introduced new layers of expression, broadening the festival's artistic diversity while fostering meaningful cultural exchanges. The festival became a space for creative exploration, where artists could push boundaries while maintaining respect for tradition with its prestige and reputation firmly established. Many performances during this period featured unique thematic presentations, narrative storytelling, and experimental choreography, allowing artists to reimagine classical forms in fresh and compelling ways. The Konark Music and Dance Festival had successfully embraced change without compromising its cultural integrity. Its ability to adapt and innovate ensured that it remained relevant to modern audiences while continuing to celebrate India's timeless artistic heritage by 2020.

Virtual Adaptations during the Pandemic : 2021

The COVID-19 pandemic brought unprecedented challenges to the global arts and cultural landscape, and the Konark Music and Dance Festival was no exception. The festival was forced to re-imagine its traditional format with travel restrictions and safety concerns preventing in-person gatherings, rather than halting its long-standing legacy, the organizers embraced digital innovation, introducing virtual performances and live streaming to ensure its continuity and global accessibility. The festival transitioned to an online platform, allowing artists to perform from various locations across India and the world. These performances were broadcast live, ensuring that audiences could witness the grandeur of Indian classical dance and music from the safety of their homes. The shift to virtual programming expanded the festival's reach beyond its traditional physical attendees. For the first time, viewers from different continents—many of whom may never have had the opportunity to attend in person—could experience the enchantment of Konark's artistic brilliance. This global digital presence significantly increased the festival's visibility and introduced Indian classical arts to new and diverse audiences. While the transition to an online format posed technical and logistical hurdles, it also opened new possibilities for the festival's future. Pre-recorded performances, artist interviews, and interactive Q&A sessions became integral components, fostering greater audience engagement and ensuring that the festival remained a dynamic and immersive cultural experience despite physical limitations. The Konark Music and Dance Festival had not only survived the challenges of the pandemic but had also pioneered a new way of experiencing classical Indian arts. This phase reinforced the festival's resilience and commitment to artistic excellence, proving that even in times of crisis, culture and tradition could find new ways to thrive and inspire by the end of 2021.

The Grand Return to an Offline Festival :2022

The Konark Music and Dance Festival made a much-anticipated return to in-person performances in 2022, symbolizing a revival of cultural exchange in the post-pandemic era. The festival's reopening was met with enthusiasm, as artists and audiences alike rejoiced in the opportunity to experience the magic of live performances once again. The transition back to an offline format restored the festival's essence of immersive cultural engagement, where the grandeur of classical dance and music could be fully appreciated in its authentic setting. Performances took place against the majestic backdrop of the Sun Temple, allowing audiences to witness the rich artistry, vibrant costumes, and intricate expressions of dancers in person. This return to physical stages rekindled the festival's intimate and communal atmosphere, which had been absent during its virtual editions. Despite the festival's successful return, several challenges persisted. Securing adequate funding remained a primary concern, as the pandemic had significantly impacted sponsorships and financial backing for cultural events. Additionally, maintaining high artistic standards, accommodating new audience expectations, and ensuring seamless execution after a year-long hiatus required strategic planning and renewed efforts from organizers. The festival not only sought to restore its pre-pandemic grandeur but also to adapt to the evolving interests of modern audiences. This meant curating performances that honoured classical traditions while embracing contemporary innovations, ensuring that the event remained relevant and engaging for both long-time patrons and newer generations of spectators. The Konark Music and Dance Festival had successfully reaffirmed its significance as a premier cultural event, overcoming pandemic-related obstacles and ushering in a new era of artistic vibrancy and global cultural exchange by the end of 2022

Global Outreach and Expansion : 2023-24

The Konark Music and Dance Festival continues to grow and evolve, embracing new artistic influences while remaining firmly rooted in India's classical dance and music traditions. As one of the most prestigious cultural events in the world, the festival has expanded its reach, drawing renowned artists, scholars, and audiences from across the globe. While the festival remains dedicated to classical Indian dance and music, it has also incorporated contemporary elements to attract younger audiences and foster greater artistic experimentation. Collaborations between classical and modern art forms, thematic performances, and experimental choreography have introduced new dimensions to traditional storytelling, ensuring that the festival remains dynamic and relevant. The festival has solidified its position as a key platform for international artistic collaboration. Artists from different cultural backgrounds participate in fusion performances, blending Indian classical traditions with global influences, thereby broadening the festival's appeal while maintaining its authentic essence. With its spectacular setting at the UNESCO-listed Sun Temple in Konark, the festival has become a major attraction for cultural tourists. Visitors from across the world travel to witness the magnificence of India's classical arts, contributing to the promotion of Odisha's rich cultural heritage and tourism industry. The Konark Music and Dance Festival remains a beacon of artistic excellence, continuing its mission to preserve, promote, and innovate within the realm of Indian classical arts. Through its unwavering commitment to cultural heritage and artistic evolution, it reaffirms its position as a leading global platform for dance, music, and cultural dialogue.

Role in Promoting Indian Classical Dance Forms

Indian classical dance originated around 200 BCE in India as a form of joyful and celebratory expression, often dedicated to Hindu deities. Many performances are choreographed to narrate stories of gods, epics, and historical events. Each style of Indian classical dance is vibrant, expressive, and deeply spiritual. These performances commonly take place at festivals, universities, cultural events, and other significant gatherings.

Dancers specializing in Indian classical dance are usually professionals who have devoted years to mastering their respective styles. During performances, they move in sync with the rhythm of the accompanying music or song. In certain styles, such as Kathak, dancers wear bells (ghungroos) around their ankles to enhance the rhythmic impact of their footwork. The dancer embodies the character they portray, following a structured composition while establishing an emotional connection with both the story and the audience.

Traditional attire plays a crucial role in classical dance performances. Female dancers typically wear colourful, handcrafted costumes such as sarees, lehengas, or kurtas, often intricately embroidered and embellished with beads. These outfits are worn barefoot. Accessories include elaborate jewellery such as necklaces, earrings, nose rings, rings, bracelets, and anklets—sometimes adorned with bells that chime with each rhythmic stomp. The costume is often complemented by a headpiece or a scarf, depending on the dance style. Dancers also wear striking facial makeup, not only to enhance their visibility on stage but also to fully embody their character.

Indian classical dance, or *Shastriya Nritya*, is a broad

term encompassing various regionally specific classical dance traditions of India. These traditions are deeply rooted in Hindu musical theatre and are based on the principles outlined in the Sanskrit text *Natya Shastra*. The number of recognized Indian classical dance styles varies, with different scholars and sources citing between six, eight, twelve, or even more styles.

The primary institution for the preservation of Indian performing arts, the Sangeet Natak Akademi, officially recognizes eight classical dance forms: Bharatanatyam, Kathak, Kuchipudi, Odissi, Kathakali, Sattriya, Manipuri, and Mohiniyattam. Additionally, the Indian Ministry of Culture includes Chhau, bringing the total to nine. Some scholars, such as Drid Williams, further expand the list by including Chhau, Yakshagana, and Bhagavata Mela.

Each classical dance form originates from a distinct region or state of India. Like Bharatanatyam originates from Tamil Nadu in southern India, Odissi from Odisha on the east coast, and Manipuri from the north-eastern state of Manipur. The music accompanying these performances features compositions in various Indian languages, including Hindi, Malayalam, Meitei (Manipuri), Sanskrit, Tamil, Odia, Telugu, and Assamese. These diverse styles, costumes, and expressions reflect both the unity and rich cultural diversity of Indian classical dance.

The Konark Dance Festival, held annually in the picturesque coastal town of Konark, Odisha, India, has evolved over the years into a globally recognized cultural event that celebrates the rich heritage and artistic traditions of the region. This festival, rooted in the intricate and captivating dance forms of Odisha, has become a sustainable landmark that not only preserves the cultural legacy of the state but also attracts audiences from around the world. It serves as a platform for renowned and emerging classical dancers to showcase their artistry, ensuring the continued appreciation and evolution of these and the preservation of cultural heritage, particularly intangible aspects like traditional dance, has become an urgent concern in the era of globalization. As the world becomes increasingly interconnected, the challenge of maintaining and promoting unique cultural traditions while adapting to modern influences has intensified. Odisha , with its rich and diverse cultural history initiatives highlight how cultural festivals can act as both guardians of tradition and catalysts for innovation, India, with its rich and diverse cultural history, stands as a vibrant example of how ancient heritage can be sustained in contemporary times. The Konark Music Dance Festival, held annually against the iconic backdrop of the 13th-century Sun Temple in Odisha, exemplifies this effort. Traditional Indian dance forms such as Bharatanatyam, Kathak, and Odissi are not merely artistic expressions but also profound representations of the cultural identity and heritage of different regions within the country. These classical dance styles encapsulate centuries of history, mythology, and spirituality, reflecting India's vast and intricate cultural mosaic. However, globalization presents both challenges and opportunities for the survival and evolution of these dance forms in contemporary society.

Each classical Indian dance form possesses a unique stylistic and cultural essence, deeply rooted in the religious and artistic traditions of its region: Bharatanatyam (Tamil Nadu) originated in South Indian temples as a Hindu devotional dance, traditionally performed as an offering to deities. It is known for its fixed upper torso, bent legs, intricate footwork, expressive hand gestures (mudras), and facial expressions (abhinaya) that vividly depict mythological narratives.

Kathak (North India), once a storytelling tradition performed by itinerant bards, evolved into a court dance under the Mughal influence. It is characterized by intricate footwork, rapid spins, graceful arm movements, and rhythmic compositions (tukras and tihais) performed with ankle bells (ghungroos) to accentuate the beats. Odissi (Odisha) has its origins in temple rituals, where it was performed as an act of religious devotion. It is recognized for its fluid, lyrical movements; elaborate postures, and expressions that depict scenes from Hindu scriptures, particularly Lord Jagannath's legends and episodes from the Ramayana and Mahabharata.

These dance forms are meticulously taught and practiced, often passed down through Guru-Shishya Parampara (the teacher-disciple tradition), ensuring the transmission of their intricate techniques and cultural narratives across generations. While globalization has led to a greater global audience and appreciation for Indian classical dance, it has also introduced challenges such as commercialization, dilution of traditional techniques, and a shift in cultural priorities. Many younger generations are gravitating toward contemporary dance styles, leading to a decline in the number of practitioners dedicated to traditional forms. Additionally, modernization has altered performance spaces, shifting dance from temples and royal courts to stages, television, and digital platforms.

However, globalization also provides unique

opportunities. Increased international recognition through festivals, collaborations, digital media, and online learning platforms has allowed Indian classical dance to reach a wider audience. Cultural exchange programs and global performances have enabled artists to share the beauty of these traditions with the world, ensuring their continuity in a modern context. This festival plays a pivotal role in sustaining and revitalizing classical dance traditions.

The Konark Music and Dance Festival has played a significant role in elevating the global status of Indian classical dance by creating a prestigious platform that attracts international audiences, artists, and cultural enthusiasts. With the rise of social media, live streaming, and digital broadcasting, the Konark Dance Festival has expanded its audience far beyond physical attendance. Performances are shared on platforms like YouTube, Facebook, and Instagram, allowing global audiences to experience the festival from anywhere in the world. This digital outreach has helped sustain interest in Indian classical dance among diaspora communities and enthusiasts worldwide. The festival serves as a cultural bridge, strengthening diplomatic and artistic ties between India and other nations. Foreign dignitaries, cultural organizations, and embassies often participate in or support the event, further enhancing India's soft power and cultural diplomacy.

The Konark Dance Festival serves as a vital platform for nurturing young talent in the field of Indian classical dance. It plays a crucial role in ensuring the continuity of classical dance traditions by introducing new generations to these art forms in a professional and highly respected setting. The exposure gained at Konark Dance Festival can open doors to further training, scholarships, and international opportunities, helping young dancers establish themselves in the world of classical performing arts.

Through its commitment to encouraging fresh talent, the Konark Dance Festival acts as a bridge between the past and the future, ensuring that the legacy of Indian classical dance thrives for generations to come.

Each year, the festival draws dance enthusiasts, scholars, tourists, and cultural connoisseurs, creating a surge in tourism that benefits various sectors. Local artisans and handicraft sellers find a thriving marketplace for their traditional crafts, such as Pattachitra paintings, silver filigree work, and handwoven textiles, which gain increased visibility and sales during the festival.

Additionally, the influx of visitors boosts hospitality services, including hotels, restaurants, and transport providers, generating employment opportunities and fostering economic growth in the region. The festival also encourages sustainable tourism, as visitors explore the surrounding heritage sites, such as the Jagannath Temple in Puri and the Chilika Lake, further enhancing Odisha's appeal as a cultural and historical destination.

By blending art, heritage, and tourism, the Konark Dance Festival not only preserves classical dance traditions but also serves as a powerful driver of economic development, ensuring that local communities benefit from the global appreciation of India's rich cultural legacy. The Konark Dance Festival is deeply intertwined with the Jagannath culture of Odisha, which holds immense spiritual and cultural significance for the people of the state. Rooted in the traditions of Lord Jagannath, the presiding deity of

Puri, this rich cultural heritage has not only been revered within India but has also gained international recognition.

The fusion of maritime heritage with Odisha's artistic traditions enhances the festival's enduring appeal, making it not just a celebration of classical dance but also a reflection of the deep-rooted traditions and lifestyles of the Odia people. Through its performances and thematic presentations, the festival highlights the narratives of Odisha's maritime history, where ancient trade routes facilitated the exchange of cultural influences, contributing to the evolution of dance, music, and storytelling traditions in the region. This interwoven history is particularly evident in the depiction of themes related to sea voyages, trade with Bali, Java, and Sumatra, and mythological tales of maritime expeditions in classical dance choreographies performed at the festival.

A key aspect of this cultural ecosystem is the contribution of local artisans, particularly from Raghurajpur, a heritage village renowned for its Pattachitra paintings, Gotipua dance, and traditional crafts. Their dedication to preserving age-old art forms directly supports the growth of dance and cultural tourism in Odisha. The involvement of these artisans not only sustains their livelihoods but also enriches the festival's visual and cultural landscape, further cementing its status as a global cultural and sustainable landmark.

The festival's growing recognition is reflected in the numerous awards and accolades bestowed upon its cultural practitioners, performers, and organizers over the years. This continued appreciation underscores the festival's role as a bridge between history and modernity, ensuring that Odisha's artistic and maritime heritage remains a source of global admiration and inspiration.

The diversity of Indian classical dance is significantly highlighted by the Konark Dance Festival, with Odissi as the focal point, aiding its revival. Major styles like Bharatanatyam, Kathak, and Kuchipudi are encompassed, while lesser-known regional forms are also promoted. Artistic excellence is encouraged through carefully selected performances, motivating artists to enhance their skills. Tradition is balanced with innovation by inviting new choreography, allowing classical dance forms to evolve and adapt over time.

To add to the preservation of India's classical traditions, several documentaries and cultural films have highlighted the Konark Dance Festival, capturing both its artistic grandeur and its role in sustaining Odisha's heritage. Produced by international filmmakers and cultural organizations, these works situate the festival within the global arts landscape, often premiering at film festivals and cultural forums where they spark curiosity and admiration for India's dance legacy.

This cultural visibility is further strengthened by the Odisha Tourism Department, which actively promotes the festival through travel fairs, brochures, and collaborations with international tourism boards. Its inclusion in global travel itineraries has steadily increased international tourist arrivals, transforming Konark into a hub of cultural tourism. Partnerships with UNESCO and other cultural institutions have further reinforced the festival's stature as a guardian of intangible cultural heritage, lending it global recognition and prestige.

The sustained media exposure and international recognition of the festival create a positive cycle of economic growth. Increased investments in hospitality, handicrafts, and cultural tourism generate employment opportunities and support regional development. Tourists visiting during the festival are also encouraged to explore other heritage sites in Odisha, such as the Jagannath Temple in Puri, Chilika Lake, and the Dhauli Peace Pagoda, extending their stay and boosting local businesses. Ultimately, the cultural prestige of Odisha is enhanced, inspiring other states in India to implement similar initiatives that celebrate and preserve their artistic heritage.

By harmonizing cultural heritage with economic sustainability, the *Konark* Dance Festival sets a benchmark for responsible cultural tourism. It not only preserves *Odisha's* artistic legacy but also ensures that local communities benefit from long-term economic growth, positioning the state as a global leader in sustainable cultural tourism. The continued success of the festival encourages investment in cultural tourism, leading to infrastructure development and the growth of small and medium enterprises (SMEs) in the region. Many seasonal job opportunities gradually transform into full-time employment as *Odisha* establishes itself as a year-round cultural and tourist destination. Furthermore, the festival's influence extends beyond its duration, as returning visitors continue to explore local heritage sites, contributing to sustained economic activity in the region.

The Konark Dance Festival is far more than an artistic event; it is a continuum of heritage, where India's classical traditions are not only preserved but also reinterpreted for new generations. By reviving forgotten dance forms, archiving performances, and nurturing young talent, the festival safeguards cultural memory while ensuring its transmission into the future. At the same time, its global recognition fosters cultural diplomacy, establishing Indian dancers as ambassadors of tradition on international stages.

Equally significant is its contribution to society at large. The festival stimulates cultural tourism, generating employment for local communities, sustaining artisans, and invigorating Odisha's economy. Through these interwoven layers—artistic excellence, heritage preservation, social empowerment, and economic growth—the Konark Dance Festival emerges as both a custodian of the past and a catalyst for the future.

In its rhythm lies not only the pulse of India's artistic spirit but also a promise: that culture, when nurtured with devotion and vision, becomes a source of knowledge, livelihood, and pride. Konark Dance Festival, therefore, is not just a festival—it is a living dialogue between history and modernity, a luminous reminder that art is the truest guardian of civilization.

References:
- Banerjee, M. (2024). *Staging Statecraft: Dance Festivals and Cultural Representations in Konark, Odisha, India.* **Arts, 13**(6), 166. https://doi.org/10.3390/arts13060166 MDPI
- Odisha Tourism. (n.d.). *Konark Dance Festival.* Retrieved August 21, 2025, from https://odishatourism.gov.in odishatourism.gov.in+1
- Konark Natya Mandap. (n.d.). *Konark Dance & Music Festival.* Retrieved August 21, 2025, from https://www.konarkfestival.com konarkfestival.com
- Incredible India. (n.d.). *Konark Festival: A celebration of dance and heritage.* Retrieved August 21, 2025,

from https://www.incredibleindia.gov.in Incredible India
- UNESCO. (n.d.). *Sun Temple, Konârak* (World Heritage listing). Retrieved August 21, 2025, from https://www.unesco.org UNESCO
- Banerji, A. (2019). *Dancing Odissi: Paratopic Performances of Gender and State*. Kolkata: Seagull Books. Seagull BooksUniversity of Chicago Press
- Sikand, N. (2016). *Languid Bodies, Grounded Stances: The Curving Pathway of Neoclassical Odissi Dance*. New York/Oxford: Berghahn Books. https://doi.org/10.3167/9781785333682 berghahnbooks.com
- Khokar, M., & Khokar, A. (2006). *The Dance Orissi*. New Delhi: Abhinav Publications.

Circuits of Living Heritage

Konark, with its unique focus on Surya, the god of the sun, is not just a monument; it is the golden centre of an expansive sacred geography. This area of Odisha's coast is a patchwork of temples, monuments, and natural features, each stitch sewn with stories of faith and artistic excellence. To travel through these places is to come into a living mandala, where stone, myth, and memory converge in cosmic geometry. At the centre of it all is the Sun Temple, a chariot of light, projecting spiritual power to the cardinal directions, attracting into its orbit the rivers, shrines, and monastic places that fill out this distinctive cultural geography.

Stepping out of the Sun Temple, one discovers that Konark opens into a whole world of marvels. The dawn rises over beaches where pilgrims bathe ritually, riverbanks are guarded by village gods, and hushed alleys wind past concealed Buddhist ruins. Every halt has its own beat and tale, yet all of them seem to loop back to the grand chariot of the Sun.

Chandrabhaga Beach – Where the first light of dawn meets the ocean, pilgrims still gather to bathe in waters once believed to cure and purify. Chandrabhaga Beach attracts both pilgrims and tourists. Located near Konark, just a few kilometres from Puri, it has also gained international recognition with India's prestigious Blue Flag certification, acknowledging it as a clean beach with world-class amenities. This certification, awarded by the Foundation for Environmental Education (FEE) headquartered in Copenhagen, Denmark, requires meeting 33 strict environmental, educational, and safety criteria. The shoreline, bordered by casuarina plantations, not only prevents erosion but also enhances the natural charm of the place. Uniquely, stretches of the road, river, and sea here run parallel, creating a picturesque view that captivates visitors. A pause at Chandrabhaga is often described as a great fatigue-healer—both for body and spirit—making it an essential part of the Konark experience. Yet, the charm of Chandrabhaga extends beyond its shorelines. Beneath its waters lies a lesser-known treasure which is called coral reefs.

Coral Reefs: The beach is renowned for its thriving reefs, forming an underwater ecosystem built by coral polyps bound together with calcium carbonate. These fragile marine habitats, overseen by the Ministry of Environment, Forest and Climate Change and protected under the Coastal Regulation Zone (CRZ) Notification of 1991, are legally safeguarded as CRZ-1 areas. Scuba diver Sabir Bux, identified 60 different coral species here making the site not only a spiritual and scenic retreat but also an ecological sanctuary. Travelling further along the Puri-Konark Marine Drive, the coastal landscape reveals another gem—Balighai Sea Beach.

Balighai Sea Beach: Located about 8 kilometres from the sacred city of Puri, Balighai enchants visitors with its golden sunrises and fiery sunsets. On full moon nights, the beach becomes even more magical as its white sands shimmer under the moonlight, giving it an almost ethereal glow. The casuarina groves, lining much of its stretch, provide a serene backdrop to this relatively isolated spot, where visitors can enjoy solitude away from crowds. Unlike Chandrabhaga, Balighai offers a touch of adventure with water sports like parasailing and boating facilities, inviting travellers to explore the vast expanse of the sea. Together, these coastal jewels—Chandrabhaga with its sacred resonance and reefs, and Balighai with its tranquil beauty and adventure—add layers of meaning to the Konark experience, blending spirituality, ecology, and leisure in a seamless journey. Many migratory birds can also be seen during the winter months, so it is safe to say that the beach gives you an eye-pleasing opportunity to witness gorgeous feathery friends and wonderful species of turtles. Near the Nua Nai River, this beach's scenic beauty attracts numerous tourists for picnics and boat rides. Visitors can experience the unique blend of the calm river meeting the turbulent sea. Just beyond it lays the Bali-Harina Sanctuary, where herds of graceful deer roam freely amid casuarina groves. The sanctuary, apart from being a quiet retreat into nature, also hosts the Turtle Research Centre, which plays a vital role in conserving the endangered Olive Ridley turtles that nest along Odisha's coast. This combination of wildlife and conservation gives the region a unique ecological character, reminding visitors that Konark's heritage is not only cultural but also deeply environmental.

Baliharachandi: A little farther stands Baliharachandi, a site where spirituality meets scenic grandeur. Famous for the temple of Goddess Mahisamardini Durga, revered locally as Harachandi, the shrine embodies the protective spirit of the sea. Fisherfolk and sailors regard her as the guardian deity of water and navigation, offering prayers before setting sail. Just 200 meters from the temple, a small river meets the sea, crossed by boat for a modest fare, opening onto a vast sandy dune fringed with casuarina trees—an idyllic picnic spot. With its golden sands, turbulent waves, and casuarina backdrop, Baliharachandi Beach is not only a sacred destination but also a popular spot for adventurous tourism, particularly swimming in the restless sea.

Kuruma: From the roaring sea to the quiet whispers of the past, the journey next leads inland to Kuruma, a lesser-known but historically significant Buddhist site, Located only 6.5 km from the Sun Temple, this tranquil village setting contrasts sharply with Konark's grandeur. Excavations conducted in the mid-1970s unearthed brick structures, ovens, and a series of small rooms or cells, possibly monastic in nature, surrounding a central courtyard. Though only partially excavated the finds—dated to the 9th–10th centuries A.D.—hint at Kuruma's role in Odisha's Buddhist heritage. The local tank, called *Dharma Pokhari* (the Tank of Dharma), adds to the sacred ambiance. Interestingly, scholars link the name "Kuruma" to references in ancient texts, including a 1015 A.D. manuscript in Cambridge University Library that illustrates the Kuruma Stupa of Odradesha. Today, the site stands not merely as ruins but as a quiet reminder of Odisha's layered spiritual traditions, where Hinduism and Buddhism once coexisted in proximity. There are other ancient texts that may provide links to *Kuruma.* The famous Chinese Buddhist monk-scholar *HiuenT'sang* (also known as *Husan Tsang and*

Xuanzang) travelled extensively throughout northern India between 634 and 645 A.D., and some scholars believe that one of the Buddhist *stupa* sites he describes in his journal is that of *Kuruma*.

Although multiple monasteries were established at Buddhist sites near the *Jajpur* and Cuttack districts of modern-day *Odisha, Kuruma* is the only monastery presently known near the coast. One also has to consider that the coastline has dramatically changed over the centuries, and this site may have been very close to the shoreline at one point.

Set on raised ground between the excavation area and the tank is a small, unassuming single-storied brick building, It is believed recently it is built by the ASI to replace a corrugated tin shed. Inside this building is the real gem of *Kuruma*. The brick building primarily houses four carved images: the crowned Buddha seated in *Bhumisparsa* Mudra, *Padmapani Avalokitesvara, Yamantaka Heruka*, and a *Tribikram* idol. All of these images are jointly worshiped as '*Yamadharma*' by the local villagers and were found on the banks of the nearby tank before excavations commenced on the site. The huge Buddha depicted in *Bhumisparsa* Mudra is particularly unusual due to the elaborate ornaments on his body: the crown on his head, necklace, arm anklets, and leg lace. This is currently believed to be unique among any Buddha idols in Odisha.

Buddha Statue at Kuruma

Kurumaiswara Temple, Kuruma

Close to the Buddhist site of Kuruma stands the Kurumaiswara Temple, dedicated to Lord Shiva but marked by strong Shakta influences. The presiding deity, MatsyaVarahi, is depicted with a boar's face and pot-bellied body, holding a fish and a bowl while seated on a buffalo mount.

The temple departs from the conventional *rekhadeula* style, adopting instead a semi-cylindrical Khakhara design, linking it to Chaurasi'sVarahi Temple and Bhubaneswar's VaitalDeula. Its sculptural program includes Ramayana scenes such as the golden deer episode, Sita's abduction, Jatayu's slaying, and the construction of the bridge to Lanka.

Here, Varahi is worshipped through tantric rituals, including daily fish offerings, highlighting the temple's dual importance as a site of religious practice and archaeological value.

Ramachandi Temple

Situated along the Puri–Konark Marine Drive Road, on the banks of the Kushabhadra River where it meets the Bay of Bengal, the Ramachandi Temple is one of the most revered shrines of the region. Dedicated to Goddess Ramachandi, regarded as the presiding deity of Konark, the temple is both a sacred site and a scenic retreat. Unlike the towering Sun Temple, its sanctity lies in intimacy and natural surroundings, drawing both pilgrims and travellers seeking tranquillity. It is also counted among the famous Shakti Pithas of Odisha, where devotees, especially during the month of *Ashwina*, offer *bali* (sacrifices) to the goddess. A popular legend narrated in the *Ramachandi–Kalapahad*

Upakhyana adds layers of myth to its worship. Kalapahad, a 17th-century iconoclast, after destroying the Sun Temple, attempted to demolish Ramachandi's shrine. The Goddess, disguised as a maidservant (*Maluni*), tricked him and escaped into the Kushabhadra River. Later, she appeared in the dream of a priest and instructed him to establish the temple at its present site. Today, both pilgrims and visitors flock to the temple to seek her blessings and to enjoy the serene beauty of the surrounding beach and river estuary.

Varahi Temple, Chaurasi

About 27 km from Konark, at Chaurasi, stands the Varahi Temple, an exquisite monument of the Khakhara style (Gaurichara variety), unique to Odisha. Built during the Somavamsi period in the early 10th century, it predates the Sun Temple and represents an older and more traditional architectural style. The sanctum enshrines Goddess Varahi, depicted with a boar's face and a woman's body, seated in *lalitasana* on a pedestal. She holds a fish in her right hand and a *kapala* (skull cup) in her left. Her pot-bellied form is believed to symbolize the cosmic womb, containing the universe within. Famous as the beauty of the Prachi Valley, careful restoration work has been done here. The ancient, 9th century temple is dedicated to Goddess Varahi, the female counterpart of Varaha, the boar incarnation of Vishnu. One among the Sapta-matrikas group of Vaishnavi, Maheswari, Brahmani, Indrani, Kaumari and Chamunda, this is a rare temple dedicated to Varahi alone. Varahi is an incarnation of Bhu Devi. Varahi is worshipped by three practices of Hinduism: Shaivism (devotees of Shiva), Vaishnavism (devotees of Vishnu), and especially Shaktism (goddess worship). She is usually worshipped at night, using secretive Vamamarga Tantric practices. The Buddhist goddesses Vajravārāhī and Marichi have their origins from the Hindu goddess Varahi.

There are intricate carvings all over the temple walls, with number of erotic panels suggesting tantric rites. The Varahi temple of Chaurasi is decorated with both cult images as well as non-iconic figures. The central niches of the bada houses the parshvadevata images of Ganesha and Surya. The images of Surya and Ganesha are the parshvadevatas of western (back) and southern sides of the bada respectively.

The temple's sculptural program is remarkable for its elegance, balance, and variety. The Jagamohana, with its seven tiers of *pidhas*, is adorned with figural and arabesque motifs, while wall reliefs depict episodes from the *Ramayana*, such as the abduction of Sita and the slaying of Vali. Within the sanctum and subsidiary niches, multiple images of Varahi appear in different iconographic postures, reinforcing her tantric associations. Locally revered as MatsyaVarahi, she continues to be worshipped through tantric rituals, including daily fish offerings. Architecturally and spiritually, the Varahi Temple of Chaurasi is considered the most significant monument of the Prachi Valley, making it a treasure for devotees, scholars, and art historians alike.

The Chaurashi Temple stands as a remarkable testament to Odisha's deep and ancient association with the cult of the Sacred Feminine, an enduring tradition that predates the later waves of Vaishnavism, Shaivism, and the broader process of Sanskritisation. The region's spiritual landscape has long been shaped by Tantric practices and Shakti worship, which permeated not only Hinduism but also left profound imprints on Jainism and Buddhism. These influences contributed to the emergence of new sects and interpretations within both faiths, reflecting a vibrant cross-fertilization of spiritual ideas.

What makes this heritage particularly fascinating is the syncretic veneration of Goddess Varahi, who, across different periods of history, has been worshipped as a Hindu deity, a Jaina Yakshini, and a Buddhist Vajrayogini. This fluidity of identity underscores Odisha's unique spiritual ethos—one that transcends rigid sectarian boundaries and celebrates the Divine Feminine in her many forms and manifestations.

Amareswara Shiva Temple, Amareswar Village

Situated about 5 km from Konark, the Amareswara Shiva Temple is a lesser-known yet historically significant shrine dedicated to Lord Shiva. Though smaller in scale compared to the grand Sun Temple, it is believed to have been constructed around the same period, making it an essential part of the region's temple heritage.

The temple follows the Kalinga architectural style, characterized by the traditional *rekhadeula* (curvilinear tower). Built with locally available laterite and sandstone, the structure consists of a sanctum (*garbhagriha*) housing a Shiva Lingam and a small *jagamohana* (assembly hall) in front of it. Though modest in scale, the temple features Shaivite motifs and carvings reflecting Odisha's artistic traditions. Sculptural panels depict scenes from the *Ramayana* and *Mahabharata*, while figures of celestial dancers (*apsaras*), divine musicians, and forms of Shiva such as Nataraja and Ardhanarishvara adorn its walls. Motifs of serpents (*nagas*), floral decorations, and guardian figures also appear, though some have eroded with time. The temple remains an important pilgrimage centre, especially during MahaShivaratri, when special rituals and celebrations take place.

Gangeswari Temple, Bayalish Bati

Situated in Bayalish Bati, near Gop (approximately 35 km from Puri), the Gangeswari Temple dates to the 13th century CE. Built of sandstone on a laterite foundation, it exemplifies the Pancharatha style of Kalingan architecture. The temple is adorned with carvings of Chamunda, Ashtadikpalakas, nayikas, animals, hunting, and social scenes. Of note is the four-armed Varahi as Parsvadevi, holding a bowl of blood, dagger, and shield. The sanctum houses a four-armed Mahishamardini, while the interior walls are decorated with painted motifs. The temple continues to function as a living shrine, with priests residing within the complex. Set amid lush countryside, Gangeswari Temple provides a peaceful counterpoint to the crowded Sun Temple of Konark. It has a unique entrance gate and exquisite sculptures like Konark. A beautiful image of Goddess Varahi as a parshvadevi, image of Lord Indra on his Airavat elephant, captivating stone carvings depicting stories make this temple special. Images of Naga-purusha and Naga-kanya are also found here.

Gangeswari Temple

Among the many fascinating sculptural depictions adorning the walls of this temple, one particularly rare and remarkable image is that of the Muchalinda Buddha. The presence of this image within the Gangeswari Temple—dedicated to the presiding deity who served as the Iṣṭa Devi of the Ganga dynasty—is especially intriguing. The Ganga rulers were known patrons of Vaishnavism, yet the inclusion of a Buddhist motif such as the Muchalinda Buddha suggests a subtle but significant Tantric undercurrent that permeated the region's religious milieu. According to Buddhist lore, Muchalinda is the name of a Nāga, a divine serpent being, who emerged from his abode to shield the meditating Gautama Buddha from the fury of a storm shortly after his enlightenment. Coiling his body to form a seat and spreading his hood as a canopy, Muchalinda protected the Enlightened One from the elements—a gesture that came to symbolize the harmony between nature and the awakened spirit. This sculptural inclusion also reflects the long and complex relationship between humans and serpents in the Indian subcontinent, a connection that stretches from prehistoric worship to living ritual traditions. Snakes have been venerated as both guardians and symbols of fertility, renewal, and transcendence, finding expression across mythology, folklore, agriculture, and art. The Muchalinda image thus not only enriches the temple's iconographic repertoire but also stands as a reminder of Odisha's pluralistic spiritual ethos, where Buddhist, Hindu, and Tantric traditions once intertwined seamlessly, giving rise to a deeply syncretic sacred landscape.

Though not fully established by historical evidence, the following observations hold considerable suggestive and interpretive value, especially from both historical and touristic perspectives. It is believed that Sibei Samantaray

Mahapatra, the chief architect of the magnificent Konark Sun Temple, hailed from this very village. Tradition holds that it was here the 1,200 craftsmen, engineers, and supervisors who undertook the colossal task of building Konark once resided and meticulously planned their work. The nearby Patharabuha River, now silted and blocked, is said to have played a crucial logistical role during that era—serving as a vital waterway through which stone blocks and other masonry materials were transported on log rafts to the temple site.

Adjacent to the Gangeswari Temple lies a large pond, which is believed to be the surviving remnant of this ancient river course. Standing by it, one can almost envision the industrious scene of the 13th century—the hum of activity, the rhythm of chisels, and the disciplined artistry of Odishan craftsmen shaping what would become one of the finest architectural masterpieces of India. The site today continues to evoke the symbolism, technical brilliance, and spiritual vision that defined the making of Konark, allowing visitors to connect deeply with the genius and devotion of those early temple architects.

Balukhand–Konark Wildlife Sanctuary

Stretching between Puri and Konark, the Balukhand–Konark Wildlife Sanctuary forms a lush green corridor of casuarina groves, cashew plantations, and coastal dunes, interspersed with golden beaches. Covering an area of 87 square kilometers, the sanctuary is home to a rich diversity of fauna, including blackbucks, spotted deer, jackals, and a variety of migratory and resident birds. The beaches within the sanctuary are particularly significant as nesting grounds for the endangered Olive Ridley turtles, making this an important conservation landscape.

Travelers along the Marine Drive often encounter deer grazing or birds crossing the path, slowing their journey but deepening their sense of connection to nature. The calmness of the forest, coupled with the sparkling beaches nearby, creates an atmosphere of solitude and serenity.

Beyond its spiritual and ecological attractions, the Konark region is also marked by important archaeological sites that shed light on Odisha's maritime legacy.

Manikapatna:
Located near Brahmagiri on the northeastern end of Chilika Lake, is among the most significant. Excavations reveal continuous settlement patterns from the 2nd century BCE to the 19th century CE, with pottery, coins, and artifacts indicating far-reaching trade relations. Identified with the medieval port of *Chelitalo* mentioned by the 7th-century Chinese pilgrim Xuanzang (Hiuen Tsang), Manikapatna served as a key port on the Bay of Bengal coast. The discovery of an Indo-Arabian stone anchor, along with Rouletted Ware, Kharoshthi inscriptions, semi-precious beads, and imported ceramics, confirms its role in linking Odisha not only with Bengal, Assam, and Tamil Nadu but also with the Mediterranean and Southeast Asia. Such finds underscore Odisha's pivotal role in the East–West maritime trade networks that flourished nearly two millennia ago.

Further north, the site of Khalkatpatna, excavated by the Archaeological Survey of India (1984–85), provides evidence of Odisha's active port life during the Ganga dynasty (12th–14th centuries CE). Finds include a brick-jelly floor interpreted as a loading platform, Chinese celadon ware, porcelain with blue floral motifs, stamped red ware, and copper coins. The presence of ring wells, storage jars, and finely designed ceramics of both native and foreign origin highlights Khalkatpatna's function as a vibrant hub of China–Odisha maritime exchange.

Together, Manikapatna and Khalkatpatna reveal the region's dual significance: as a religious landscape of temples and shrines, and as a maritime corridor connecting Odisha with distant lands. However, over time, the prosperity of these ports declined due to multiple factors: weak successors and political disunity, excessive taxation, and loss of royal patronage. Natural forces such as coastal erosion, shifting river courses, sedimentation, tectonic uplift, and the formation of sand bars also disrupted navigation. Ports like Konark and Balasore, once on the seashore, now lie several kilometers inland due to geological shifts.

Despite their decline, these archaeological sites highlight Odisha'sglorious maritime past and reinforce the cultural memory of the state as a land of seafarers (*Sadhabas*), who sailed across the seas carrying not just goods like spices and sandalwood but also cultural traditions and religious ideas.

Beleswar Temple (Near Puri)

The Beleswar Temple, an ancient and sacred shrine dedicated to Lord Shiva, is located near a tranquil beach, approximately 30 km from Konark and close to Puri. Though the exact period of its construction remains unrecorded, the temple is believed to be several centuries old. It holds immense religious and cultural significance, serving as an important pilgrimage site for devotees, particularly during Maha Shivaratri and other Shiva-related festivals.

The temple's serene and untouched surroundings, combined with its proximity to the sea, create a unique spiritual atmosphere that attracts both worshippers and visitors seeking peace and solitude. Unlike the more commercialized temple sites, Beleswar Temple retains an aura of tranquility, making it a perfect destination for meditation and devotion.

The temple showcases elements of the Kalinga architectural style, which is characteristic of Odisha's ancient temple-building traditions. Constructed primarily using laterite and sandstone, the temple has developed a weathered yet enduring charm over time. Its rekhadeula (curvilinear tower) structure, a hallmark of Shaivite temples in Odisha, rises gracefully over the sanctum, reflecting the architectural elegance of the region.

At the heart of the temple lies the sanctum sanctorum (garbhagriha), which houses a Shiva Lingam, the principal object of worship. This sacred chamber is connected to a jagamohana (assembly hall), a feature commonly found in Odishan temples, where devotees gather for prayers and rituals. The temple complex also includes smaller shrines dedicated to various Hindu deities, reinforcing its role as a significant spiritual centre.

While the sculptural detailing on the temple is relatively simple compared to grander temples like the Sun Temple of Konark or the Lingaraj Temple of Bhubaneswar, it still features traditional Shaivite motifs, such as:
- Nandi (the sacred bull of Shiva), often positioned in front of the sanctum.

- Serpent (naga) imagery, representing divine energy and protection.
- Bas-reliefs of various forms of Lord Shiva, including Nataraja (the cosmic dancer) and Ardhanarishvara (the fusion of Shiva and Parvati).

Over the centuries, exposure to the coastal climate has led to some erosion of the temple's intricate carvings. However, the structure remains well-preserved, retaining its spiritual and historical essence.

Beleswar Temple is deeply revered by local devotees, and it witnesses a surge in visitors during Maha Shivaratri, when grand celebrations, night-long vigils, and special rituals take place. Apart from its religious significance, the temple's coastal setting makes it a peaceful retreat for those seeking spiritual solace.

The surrounding beach and natural landscape further enhance the temple's mystical appeal. Pilgrims and tourists alike are drawn to the temple for both worship and relaxation, creating a unique blend of devotion and natural beauty. Unlike the bustling temple towns of Odisha, Beleswar offers a more secluded and introspective experience, making it an ideal spot for those looking to connect with both spiritual heritage and nature. With its historical charm, architectural simplicity, and serene location, Beleswar Temple stands as a hidden gem among Odisha's sacred sites, offering a profound sense of peace, devotion, and cultural richness

Konark: A Confluence of Multi-Thematic Circuits

Konark, often celebrated as the radiant *City of the Sun*, is not only an architectural marvel but also a living expression of Odisha's composite heritage—where art, spirituality, and ecology intertwine seamlessly. Beyond the grandeur of the Sun Temple lies an entire cultural region, pulsating with ritual life, craftsmanship, and community rhythms. To experience Konark in its entirety is to traverse through a series of thematic circuits that together illuminate the essence of Odisha—its living traditions, creative continuity, and sustainable spirit.

1. **Cultural and Performing Arts Circuit**

The Cultural Circuit of Konark epitomizes the vibrant synthesis of ritual, performance, and artistic expression that defines Odisha's living heritage. Rooted in temple traditions and folk idioms, this circuit invites travellers to experience the rhythm of the region's cultural heartbeat. The Konark Dance Festival, staged annually against the majestic backdrop of the Sun Temple, serves as the centrepiece of this circuit. Global ensembles perform classical and contemporary choreographies under the moonlit sky, transforming the temple precinct into a celestial stage. Complementing these grand performances are intimate experiences—storytelling through dance, workshops with renowned gurus, and local fairs where music and devotion merge.

Here, performance becomes prayer, and the sacred merges with the aesthetic. The cultural circuit thus connects sacred spaces, artistic expressions, and community life—revealing how history, spirituality, and creativity converge in Konark's living traditions.

2. **Fairs and Festivals Circuit**

Odisha's festivals are not isolated events but cycles of renewal that mirror the cosmic calendar. The Fairs and

Festivals Circuit offer visitors the opportunity to witness this pulsating continuum of faith and festivity. From the grandeur of the Rath Yatra at Puri to the devotional fervour of the Magha Saptami Festival and Chandrabhaga Mela near Konark, these celebrations draw together pilgrims, performers, and artisans. Ritual bathing at dawn, folk dances, devotional music, and temple processions create an atmosphere where spirituality meets spectacle. Through these experiences, visitors gain insight into how Odisha's community life remains deeply intertwined with the rhythms of nature and celestial cycles, reflecting an intimate sense of harmony between human and cosmic order.

3. Rural Tourism and Crafts Circuit

The villages surrounding Konark form the vibrant heart of Odisha's living craft traditions. The Rural Tourism and Crafts Circuit connects travellers to the artistry and hospitality of these communities. In Pipli, the intricate appliqué work that once adorned temple canopies now dazzle global admirers. Raghurajpur, the heritage village of *Pattachitra* painters and Gotipua dancers, stands as a living museum of creativity. In the coastal settlements of Nuagaon and Beleswar, traditional lifestyles coexist with agrarian rhythms and artisanal skills. Visitors can participate in hands-on workshops, enjoy Gotipua performances in courtyards, take bullock-cart rides through paddy fields, and stay in traditional homestays. The circuit thus bridges livelihood and culture, enabling travellers to engage meaningfully with the custodians of Odisha's intangible heritage.

4. **Rural and Nature Immersion Circuit**

For those seeking quiet engagement with the land, the Rural and Nature Immersion Circuit offers experiences that celebrate Odisha's pastoral beauty and sustainable ethos. In villages such as Nuagaon, Beleswar, Mirzapur etc, travellers can join in paddy harvesting, learn organic farming techniques, or cook traditional Odia cuisine using locally sourced ingredients. Evenings by the fireside are filled with folk tales, songs, and the warm camaraderie of village life. This circuit foregrounds participatory tourism, encouraging visitors to live the rhythm of the countryside while fostering appreciation for the interdependence of people and nature.

5. **Culinary and Wellness Circuit**

Odisha's philosophy of life rests upon a delicate balance between nourishment, devotion, and well-being. The Culinary and Wellness Circuit brings together these dimensions through experiences that engage both palate and spirit.

a. **Odia Culinary Circuit**

Travellers can savour the sanctified *Mahaprasad* from the Jagannath Temple kitchens, explore seaside eateries serving fresh coastal fare, or learn to prepare the quintessential *pakhala bhata* and *chhenapoda* in village homes. Each dish tells a story of ritual, community, and compassion.

b. **Wellness, Yoga, and Naturopathy Circuit**

Set against the tranquil backdrop of Chandrabhaga Beach and nearby eco-retreats, this circuit integrates yoga, meditation, Ayurveda, and naturopathy. Beach yoga at sunrise, herbal oil therapies, and guided silence retreats rejuvenate body and soul. Together, these experiences embody Odisha's philosophy of holistic balance, where food, faith, and wellness are threads of the same sacred continuum.

6. Spiritual and Mindfulness Circuit

Konark and its surrounding region form part of Odisha's sacred geography—a landscape where devotion and contemplation coexist. The Spiritual and Mindfulness Circuit weaves together the monumental and the meditative. Pilgrims trace their way from the Sun Temple at Konark to the Jagannath Temple at Puri, and onward to the serene Buddhist site of Kuruma. Along these routes, guided meditation, chanting, and storytelling sessions create spaces for inner reflection. This circuit transcends religious boundaries, reflecting Odisha's syncretic spiritual heritage, where Hindu, Buddhist, and Tantric philosophies have coexisted and enriched one another. It encourages the traveller not just to see, but to *feel*—to connect inwardly with the land's sacred resonance.

7. Maritime and Trade Heritage Circuit

Once known as ancient Kalinga, Odisha held a commanding position in maritime trade, sending voyagers across the seas to Bali, Java, and Sumatra. The Maritime and Trade Heritage Circuit revives this illustrious seafaring past.

a. Museum and Maritime Heritage Sub-Circuit

At the Archaeological Museum of Konark,

sculptures and reliefs depict boats, traders, and maritime life—visual chronicles of Odisha's global connections.

b. Coastal Village Sub-Circuit

At Chandrabhaga and nearby river-mouth villages, visitors meet traditional fishing communities, witness boat-building practices, and participate in coastal rituals that echo the ancient bond between sea and spirit.

c. Trade Heritage Sub-Circuit

Travelling through ancient port sites and exploring the maritime iconography of Konark and Chilika, visitors can reconstruct the once-bustling trade routes that positioned Odisha as both a sacred centre and a maritime hub.

Through these journeys, one discovers that Konark's narrative is not confined to land—it extends into the vast expanse of the ocean, symbolizing connection, movement, and exchange.

8. Ecotourism and Regenerative Tourism Circuit

Odisha's coastline is home to fragile yet resilient ecosystems that call for mindful engagement. The Ecotourism and Regenerative Tourism Circuits encourage responsible exploration that contributes to environmental and community well-being.

a. Coastal and Ecotourism Sub-Circuit

Sites such as the Nuanai Eco Camp, Balukhand–Konark Wildlife Sanctuary, Astaranga, and turtle nesting grounds invite travellers to observe birds, marine life, and coastal vegetation through guided eco-trails and turtle walks.

b. Regenerative Tourism Sub-Circuit

This initiative goes beyond sustainability to active restoration. In organic farming villages and eco-resorts, travellers can participate in tree planting, regenerative farming, and sustainable fishing practices—transforming travel into a force for renewal.

These circuits exemplify tourism with purpose—where nature, culture, and community coexist in harmony, fostering both awareness and stewardship.

Emerging and Complementary Circuits

To further expand the interpretive and experiential possibilities of Konark's tourism landscape, a few additional thematic circuits may be envisioned:

9. Heritage Education and Interpretation Circuit

This circuit could link museums, interpretation centres, and academic institutions through curated walks, heritage storytelling, and digital archives—promoting youth engagement and public scholarship.

10. Photography and Art Residency Circuit

By offering residencies for artists, photographers, and writers in villages like Raghurajpur and coastal Konark, this circuit could encourage creative documentation and cross-cultural exchange.

11. Architectural and Temple Heritage Circuit

Connecting Konark with nearby shrines such as Chaurashi and Gangeswari, this circuit would provide guided interpretation of Odisha's temple architecture, iconography, and evolving artistic traditions.

Together, these thematic circuits transform Konark from a single monumental destination into a multilayered cultural landscape—a region where every ritual, melody, and motif continues to breathe history. They invite travellers to move beyond observation to participation, from sightseeing to soul-seeing—where every journey becomes an act of rediscovery and reverence for Odisha's timeless spirit.

Konark emerges as more than a heritage site—it is a confluence of thematic circuits, each offering a pathway into Odisha's civilizational ethos. For travellers, these circuits are not mere itineraries but immersive experiences that allow participation in a living culture where heritage, ecology, and community remain in continuous dialogue.

At one level, the Sun Temple stands as the anchor of Odisha's historical imagination, yet around it unfolds diverse circuits—sacred geographies, coastal ecosystems, craft villages, performing arts traditions, and rural life experiences. Each circuit carries the potential to enrich both visitor experience and community livelihood, aligning with sustainable tourism goals that balance conservation, participation, and growth. For policy makers and planners, these circuits are opportunities to design models of inclusive development where heritage management is intertwined with local entrepreneurship, skill enhancement, and ecological stewardship. For the traveller, however, these pathways are journeys of discovery. They lead beyond the monument into the pulse of living traditions—rituals at temples, rhythms of Odissi dance and music, the artistry of local weavers and craftsmen, or the quiet beauty of mangroves and coastal landscapes. To walk these circuits is to join an ongoing narrative that bridges past and present, bringing the visitor into the intimate spaces of memory, identity, and creativity.

Thus, Konark must be seen not merely as a static monument but as a vibrant cultural node within Odisha's larger tourism framework—an evolving ecosystem where heritage, ecology, and community converge. To engage with Konark's circuits is both to experience the soul of Odisha and to participate in shaping a sustainable, inclusive, and resonant future for its living heritage.

References
- Archaeological Survey of India. (n.d.). *Sun Temple Konark*. Retrieved March 17, 2017, from http://www.asi.nic.in.
- Behera, K. S. (1996). *The heritage of mankind* (p. 85). New Delhi, India: Aryan Books International.
- Behera, K. S. (1996). *Konarak: The heritage of mankind* (pp. 189–191). New Delhi, India: Aryan Books International.
- Behera, K. S. (1996). *op. cit.* (p. 185).
- Behera, K. S. (1996). *op. cit.* (p. 193).
- Boner, A., Sharma, S. R., & Das, R. P. (1972). *New light on the Sun Temple Konarka: Four unpublished manuscripts relating to this temple* (p. xxxvii). Varanasi, India: Chaukhamba Sanskrit Series Office.
- Coomaraswamy, A. K. (1913). *Art and craft of India and Ceylon* (p. 75). London, England: T. N. Foulis.
- Fabri, C. L. (1974). *History of the art of Orissa* (p. 151). New Delhi, India: Orient Longman.
- Fergusson, J. (1876). *History of Indian and Eastern*

architecture (p. 106). London, England: John Murray.
- Ganguly, M. (1912). *Orissa and her remains: Ancient and medieval* (pp. 460–466). Calcutta, India: Thacker, Spink & Co.
- Ganguly, M. (1912). *Orissa and her remains: Ancient and medieval* (p. 452). Calcutta, India: Thacker, Spink & Co.
- Ganguly, M. (1912). *Orissa and her remains: Ancient and medieval* (pp. 127–128). Calcutta, India: Thacker, Spink & Co.
- Indian Archaeology. (1955–56). *Review*. Retrieved January 20, 2017, from http://www.asi.nic.in (p. 39).
- Konark Sun Temple. (n.d.). Retrieved January 15, 2017, from http://www.orissatourism.org/travel-to-orissa/konark/sun-temple-konark.html.
- Mitra, D. (1986). *Konark* (p. 107). New Delhi, India: Archaeological Survey of India.
- Mitra, D. (1986). *Konarak*. New Delhi, India: Archaeological Survey of India.
- Patra, B. (2006, April). Antiquity of ArkakshetraKonark. *Orissa Review*.
- Rath, S. S., & Rath, R. (2015). *Krupasindhu Mishra: (Konarktrans)* (pp. 93–94). Bhubaneswar, India: The Lark Books.
- Seven Wonders of India. (2017.). Retrieved March 15, 2017, from https://infogalactic.com/info/Seven_Wonders_of_India.
- Wikipedia. (2017.). *Seven Wonders of India*. Retrieved March 12, 2017, from https://en.wikipedia.org/wiki/Seven_Wonders_of_India.

Bibliography

- Altekar, S. (1938). *Position of women in India* (p. 300).
- Archaeological Survey of India. (1958). *The Ancient Monuments and Archaeological Sites and Remains Act, 1958* [PDF]. Retrieved April 17, 2015, from http://asi.nic.in
- Archaeological Survey of India. (1936). *Konarak Sun Temple*. Retrieved August 21, 2025, from http://asi.nic.in
- Archaeological Survey of India. (2025). *Konarak Sun Temple: Mithuna Sculptures*. Retrieved August 21, 2025, from http://asi.nic.in
- Archaeological Survey of India. (2025.). *Konarak, conservation*. Retrieved August 21, 2025, from http://asi.nic.in
- Achauri, S. K. (2002). Plunder of cultural and art treasures – The Indian experience. In N. Brodie & K. Walker Tubb (Eds.), *Illicit antiquities* (pp. 268–269). Routledge.
- Behera, K. S. (1996). *Konarak: The heritage of mankind*. New Delhi, India: Aryan Books International.

- Bhatkhande, V. N. (1932). *Brihaddeshi with commentary.*
- Boner, A., Sharma, S. R., & Das, R. P. (1972). *New light on the Sun Temple Konarka: Four unpublished manuscripts relating to this temple.* Varanasi, India: Chaukhamba Sanskrit Series Office.
- Bose, N. K. (1972). *Canons of Orissan architecture.*
- Chary, M. T. (2009). *India: Nation on the move.* iUniverse.
- Chenna, N. K. (2009). *Textbook of engineering geology.* Macmillan Publishers India Limited.
- Coomaraswamy, A. K. (1913). *Art and craft of India and Ceylon.* London, England: T. N. Foulis.
- Cunningham, A. (1871). *The ancient geography of India: I. The Buddhist period, including the campaigns of Alexander, and the travels of Hwen-Thsang.* London, England: Trübner & Company.
- Davidson, L. K., & Gitlitz, D. M. (2002). *Pilgrimage: From the Ganges to Graceland: An encyclopedia.* ABC-CLIO.
- Description from British Library. (2009, March 26). Retrieved from http://www.bl.uk/onlinegallery/onlineex/apac
- Fabri, C. L. (1974). *History of the art of Orissa.* New Delhi, India: Orient Longman.
- Fergusson, J. (1876). *History of Indian and Eastern architecture.* London, England: John Murray.
- Ganguly, M. (1912). *Orissa and her remains: Ancient and medieval.* Calcutta, India: Thacker, Spink & Co.
- Ghosh, M. (1967). *Nāṭyaśāstra: English translation with Sanskrit text.*

- Konark Dance Festival. (n.d.). Retrieved August 21, 2025, fromhttps://www.konarkfestival.com
- Gupta, V. K. (2019). Retrieval of Indian antiquities: Issues and challenges. *Art, Antiquity & Law, 24*(2), 101–124.
- Junghare, S. A. (2021). The architectural study of Sun Temple in India based on location, construction material, and spatial and statistical analysis study. *International Journal of Scientific & Research Publications, 3*(1), 331–338.
- Kelley, D. H., & Milone, E. F. (2011). *Exploring ancient skies: A survey of ancient and cultural astronomy*. Springer.
- Kramrisch, S. (1946). *The Hindu temple* (Vol. II). Calcutta, India: University of Calcutta.
- Mahanta, A. (2023). Dance festivals and cultural representation in Konark, Odisha, India. *Arts, 13*(6).
- Mayarani, P. (2015, December). Astronomical heritage: The Sun Temple-Konark. *Journal of the Indian Institute of Architects, 80*(12), 17.
- Mishra, M. (2015). Promotion of tourism through events: A study on Konark festival. *Orissa Review, December*, 9–12.
- Mitra, D. (1986). *Konark*. New Delhi, India: Archaeological Survey of India.
- Mitra, R. L. (1875). *The antiquities of Orissa* (Vol. 1). Calcutta, India: Wyman and Co.
- Mohapatra, R. (2023). Study on art and architectural patterns of the Sun Temple of Konark in Eastern India. *Shodhkosh: Journal of Visual and Performing Arts, 4*(1).

- O'Malley, L. S. S. (2007). *Bengal district gazetteer: Puri*. New Delhi, India: Concept Publisher.
- Odisha Tourism. (2025.). *Konark Dance Festival*. Retrieved August 21, 2025, from https://www.odishatourism.gov.in
- Patra, B. (2006, April). Antiquity of Arkakshetra Konark. *Orissa Review*.
- Prakash, P. (2023). Explained: What is the Ancient Monuments and Archaeological Sites and Remains (Amendment) Bill? *The Hindu*. Retrieved April 20, 2024, from https://www.thehindu.com
- Raghavan, V. (1956). *Abhinavabhāratī (Commentary on Nāṭyaśāstra)*.
- Rath, S. S., & Rath, R. (2015). *Krupasindhu Mishra (Konark trans)*. Bhubaneswar, India: The Lark Books.
- Reddy, K. K. (2003). *Indian history*. New Delhi, India: Tata McGraw-Hill Education.
- Rosen field, J. M. (1967). *The dynastic arts of the Kushans*. University of California Press.
- Selin, H. (2008). *Encyclopedia of the history of science, technology, and medicine in non-Western cultures* (2nd ed.). Springer.
- Sen, S. (2013). *A textbook of medieval Indian history*. New Delhi, India: Primus Books.
- Sengupta, S. (2012, September 22). Poetry in stone. *Daily Pioneer*.
- The Guru extraordinaire. (2012, May 16). *The New Indian Express*.
- The Sun Temple. (n.d.). *Tourism Department, Government of Orissa*. Retrieved May 20, 2017, from http://www.konark.nic.in

- The Sun Temple. (n.d.). *Tourism Department, Government of Orissa*. Retrieved May 20, 2017, from http://www.konark.nic.in
- Tourism Department, Government of Orissa. (n.d.). *The Sun Temple Legend*. Retrieved from http://www.konark.org/legend-konark.html
- Travelogue. (2011, July 7). Konark Sun Temple. Retrieved from http://www.premaanand-travelogue.blogspot.in/2011/07/konark-sun-temple-puri-orissa-india.html
- Wikipedia. (n.d.). *Seven Wonders of India*. Retrieved August 21, 2025, from https://en.wikipedia.org/wiki/Seven_Wonders_of_India
- UNESCO. (1984). *World Heritage List: Sun Temple, Konârak*. UNESCO.
- UNESCO World Heritage Centre. (n.d.). *Sun Temple, Konârak*. Retrieved August 21, 2025, from https://whc.unesco.org/en/list/246/
- Varghese, P. C. (2012). *Engineering geology for civil engineers*. PHI Learning Pvt. Ltd.

Black Eagle Books

www.blackeaglebooks.org
info@blackeaglebooks.org

Black Eagle Books, an independent publisher, was founded as a nonprofit organization in April, 2019. It is our mission to connect and engage the Indian diaspora and the world at large with the best of works of world literature published on a collaborative platform, with special emphasis on foregrounding Contemporary Classics and New Writing.

www.ingramcontent.com/pod-product-compliance
Lightning Source LLC
Chambersburg PA
CBHW061747070526
44585CB00025B/2821